MY ART

BY

PECHO

FLOWER PEDALS 2010

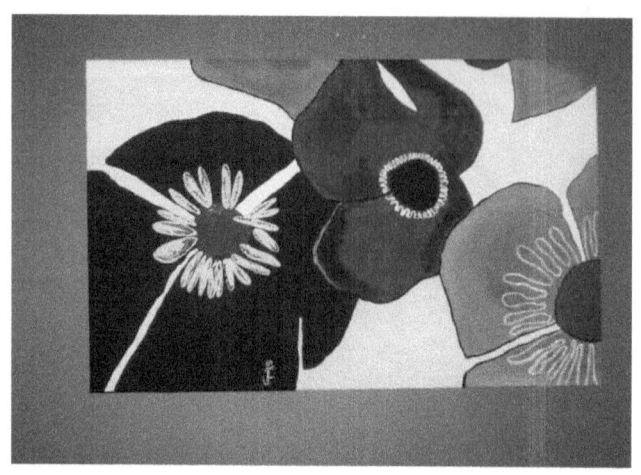

FLOWERS IN BLOOM   2011

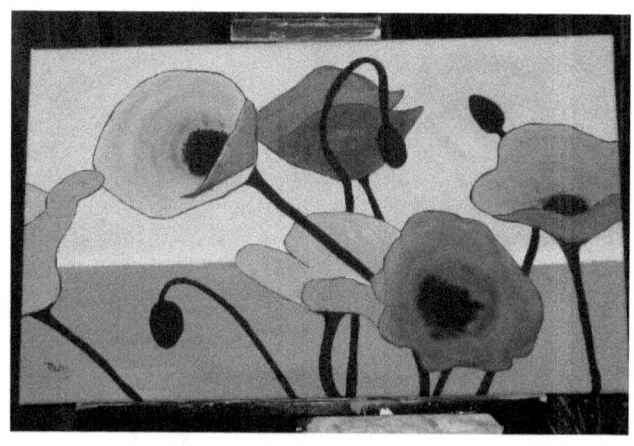

TREE OF DEATH 2011

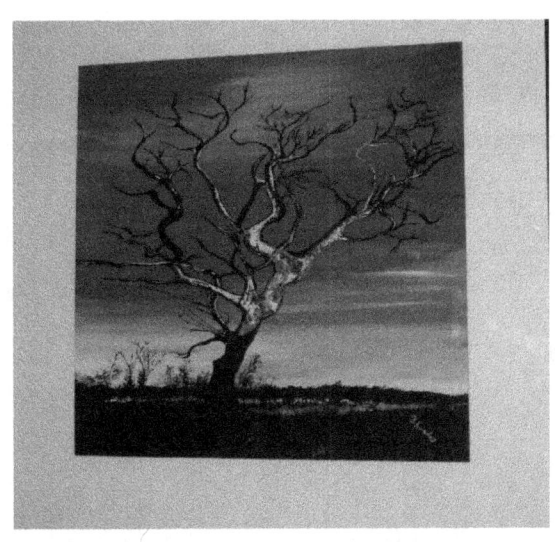

VALLEY OF BLOOMS

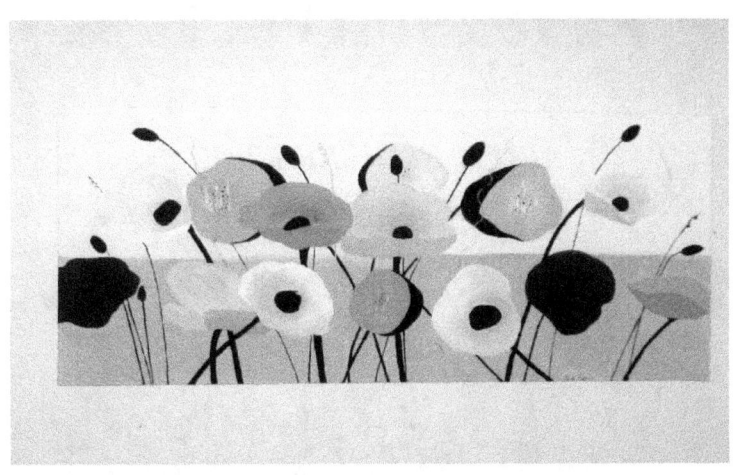

SUMMER BLOOM 2011

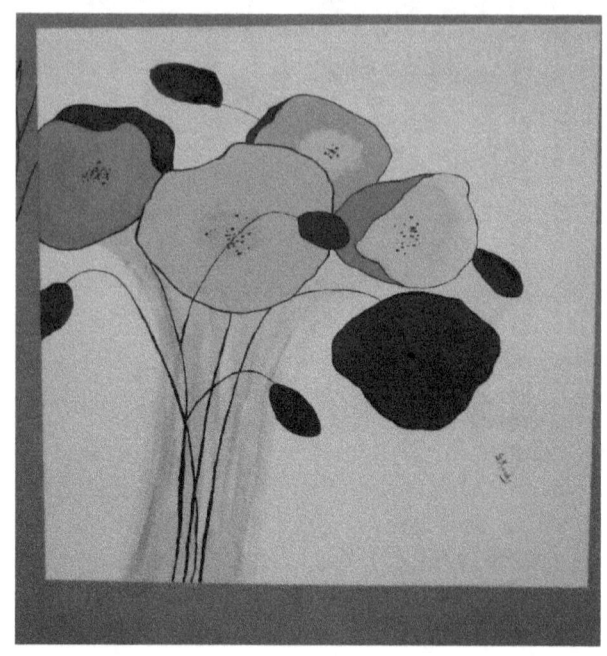

ALIEN FLOWERS 2012

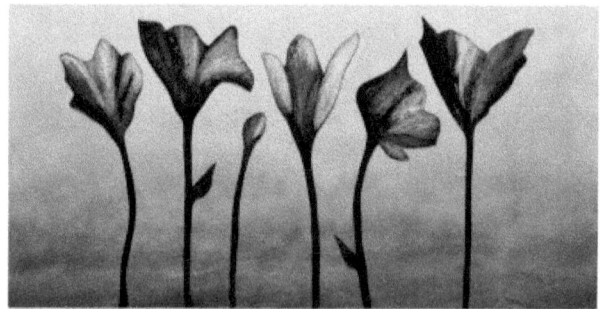

FLOWERS IN THE SUMMER 2011

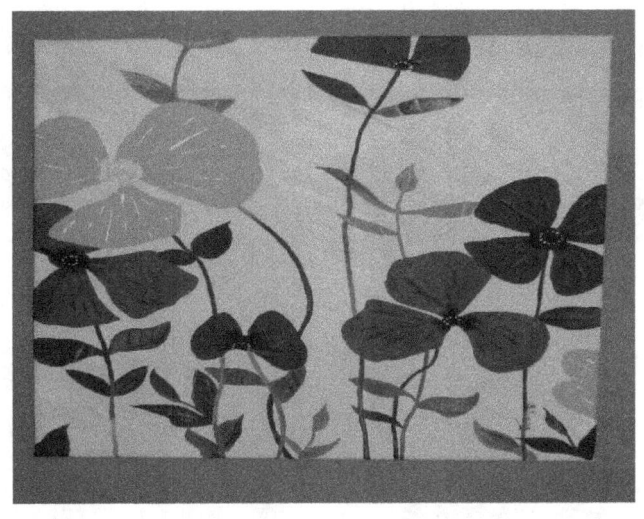

THE PEAK 2010

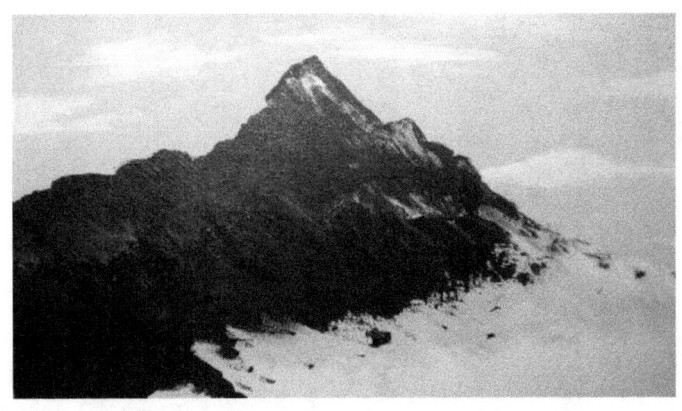

MY BIRCH TREES 2012

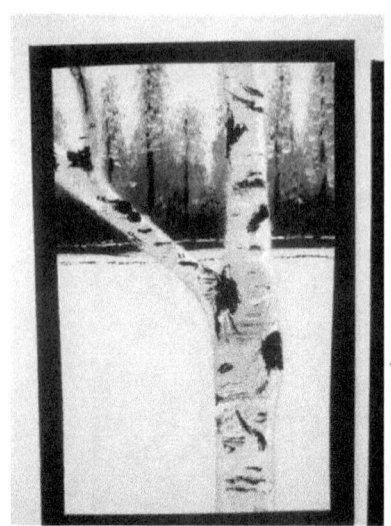
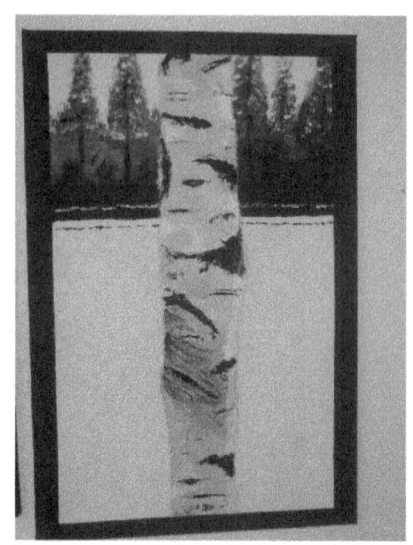
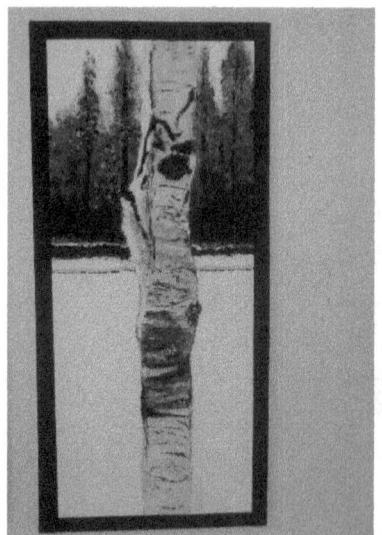
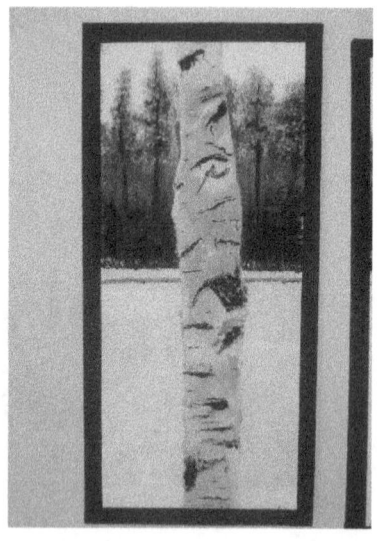

FULL BLOOM 2013

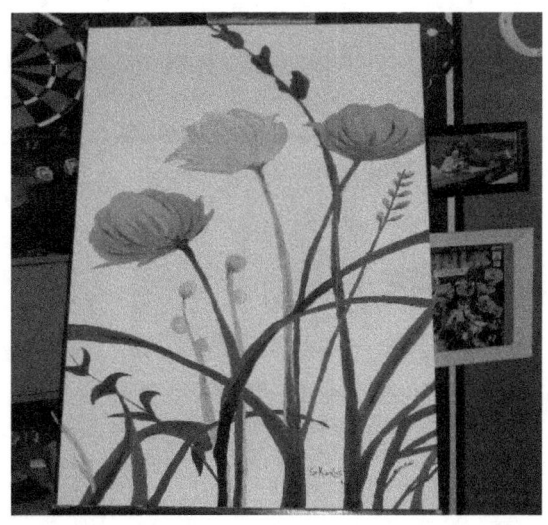

FALLING DAISIES 2013

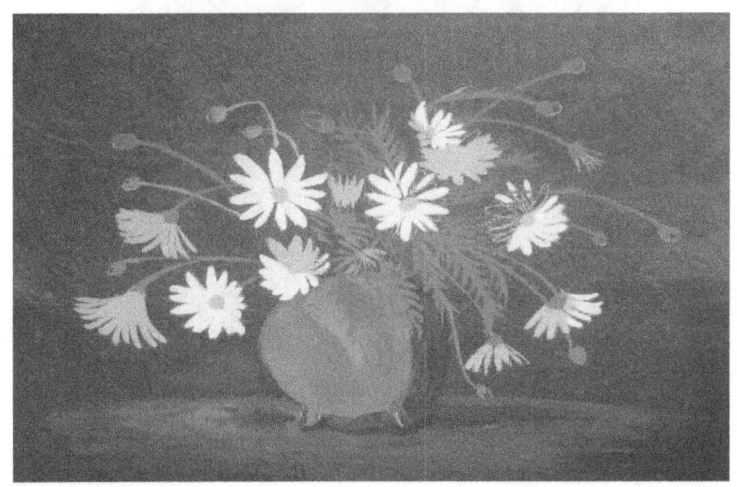

THE POND 2013

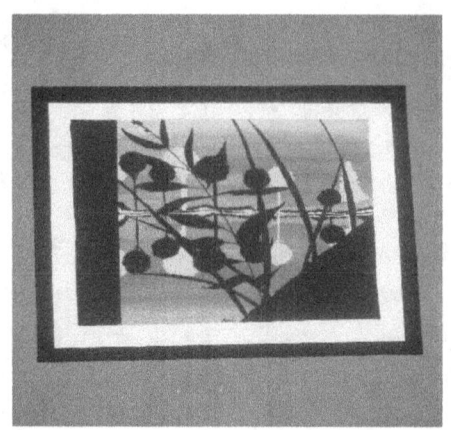

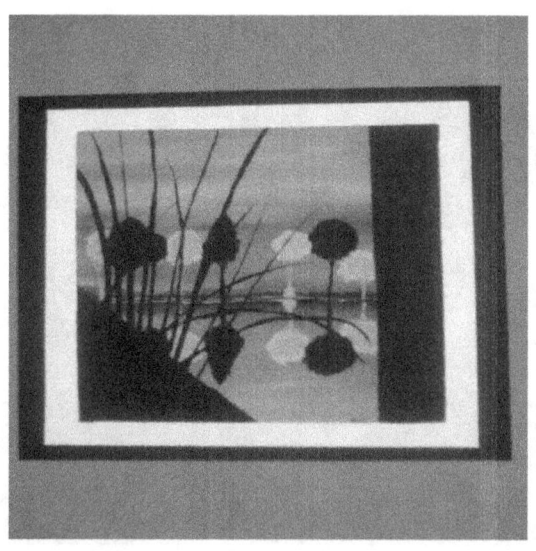

RED BURCH IN THE DARK 2013

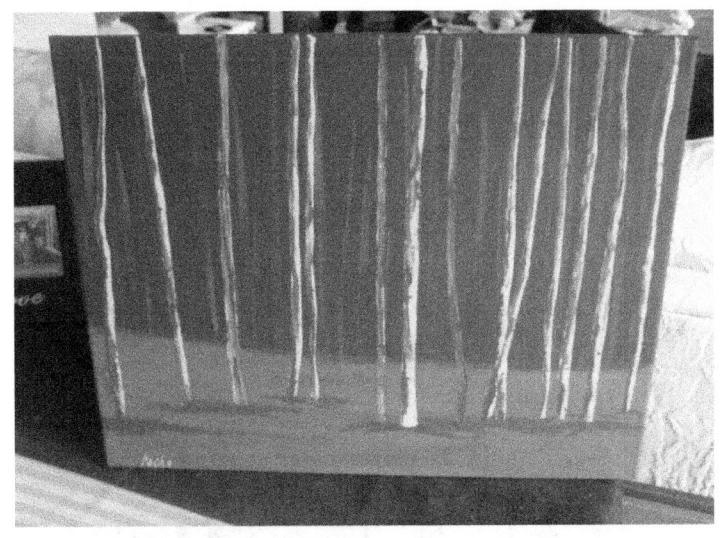

RED MOON 2013

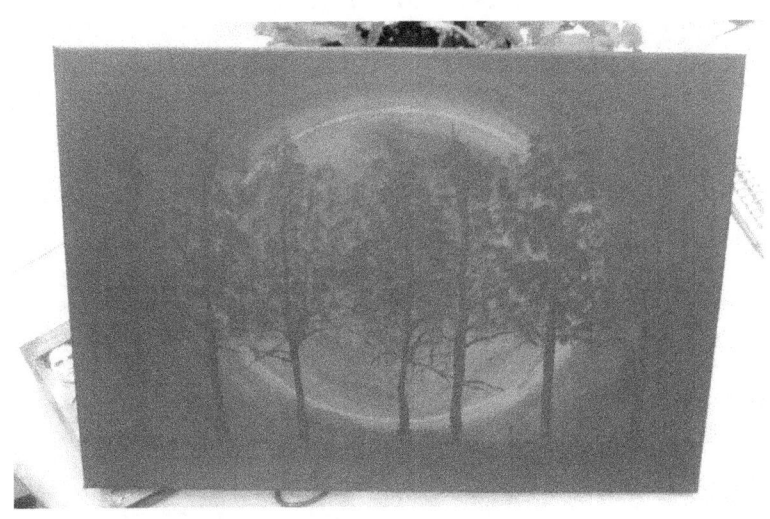

SPLIT VIEWS 2014

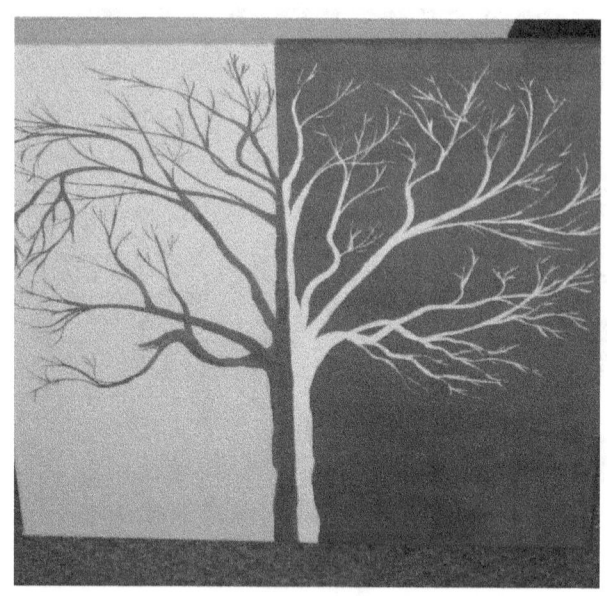

MAGNOLIA 2014

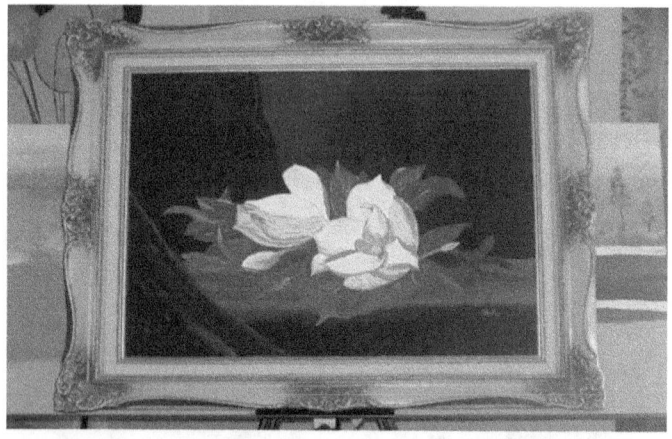

FRESH FLOWERS 2014

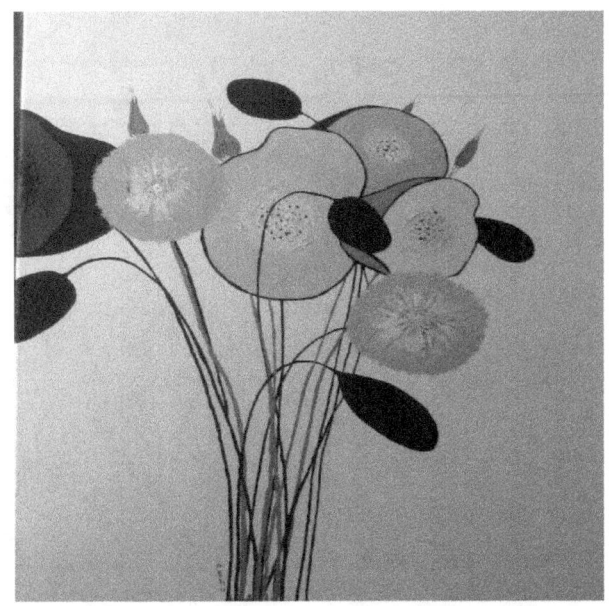

BEAUTIFUL MAGNOLIAS 2014

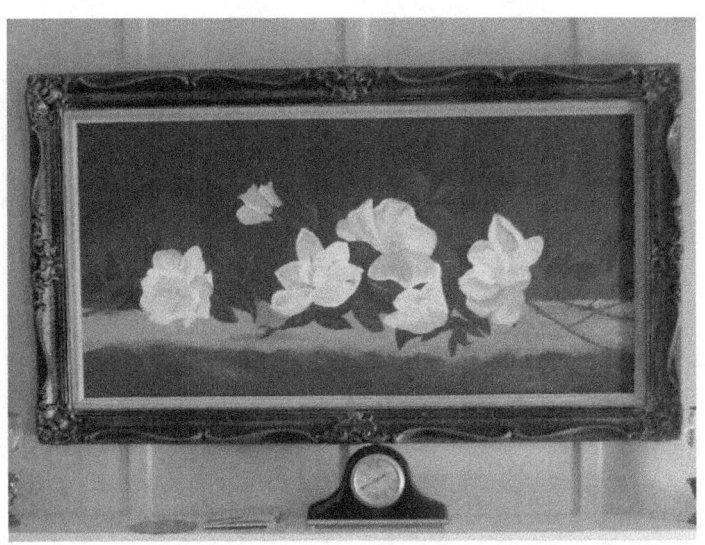

ROSES FOR MY WIFE 2013

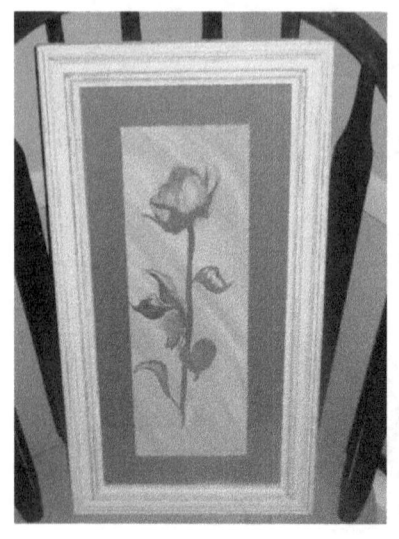 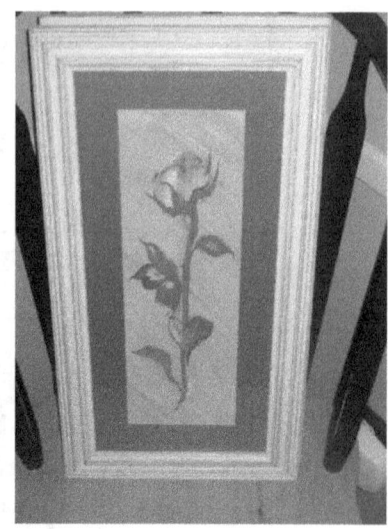

POPPI'S 2014

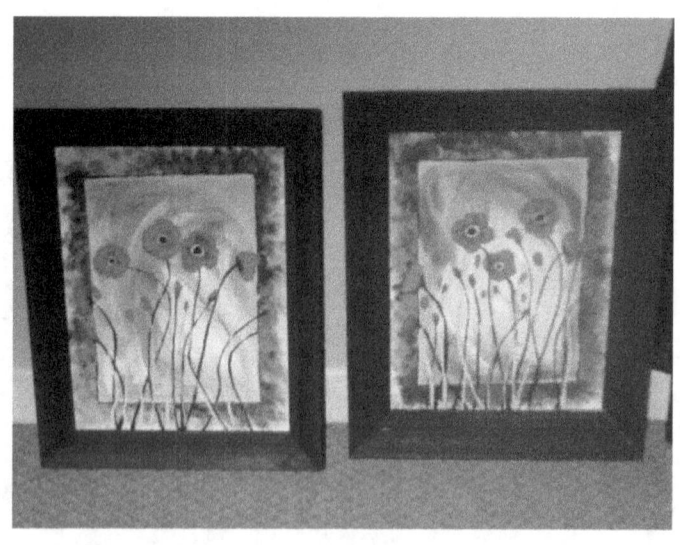

BEAUTIFUL LILLY 2014

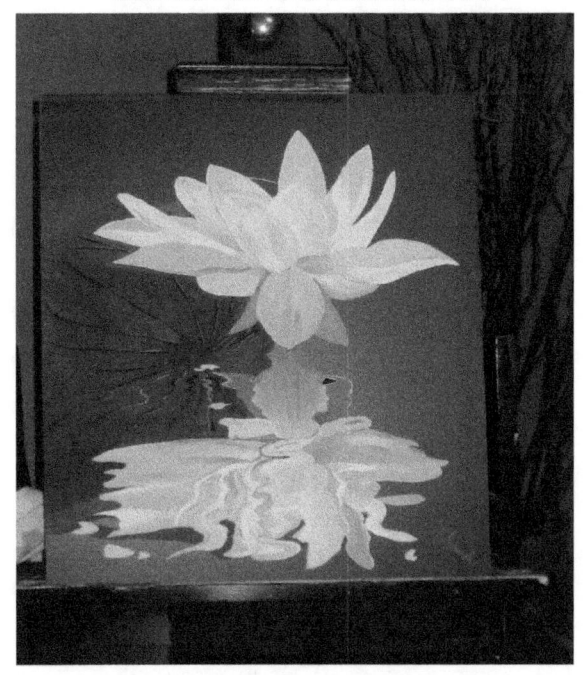

SHADOW TREES 2011

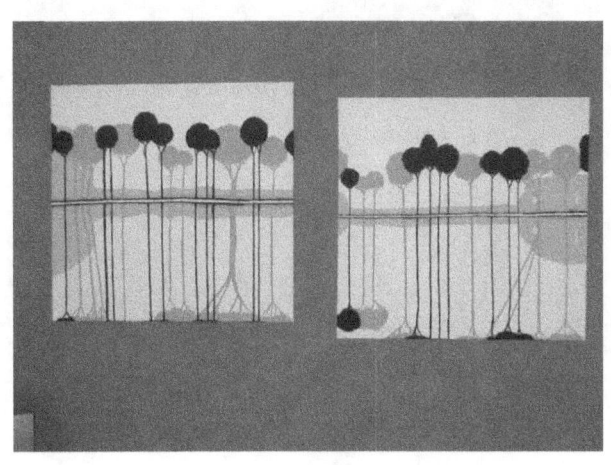

MY TREE LADY 2011

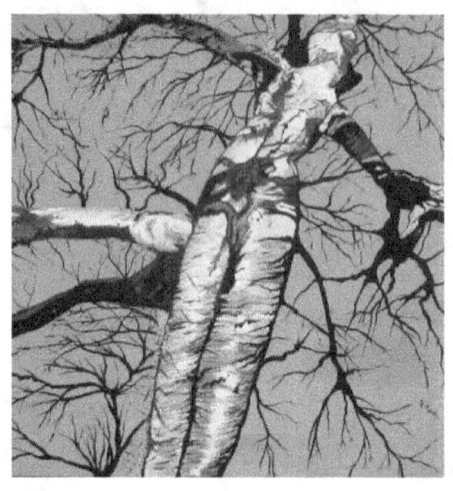

TREE IN REFLECTION 2011

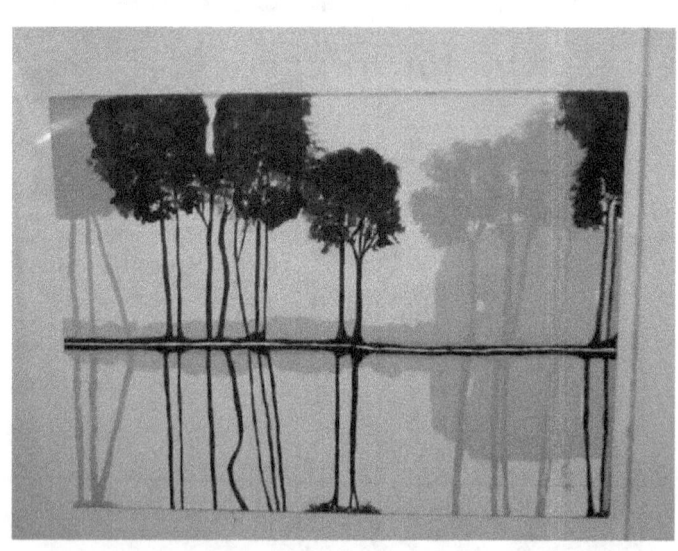

BLOOM OF THE TABLE 2013

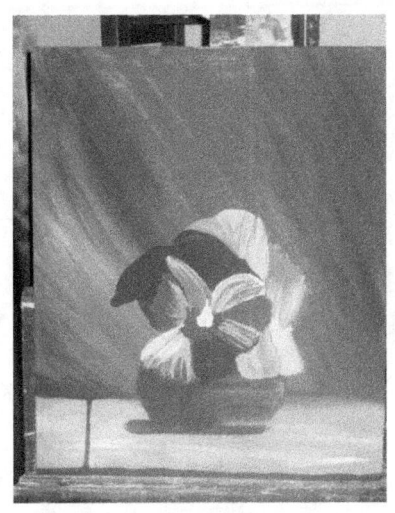

PARIS 2013

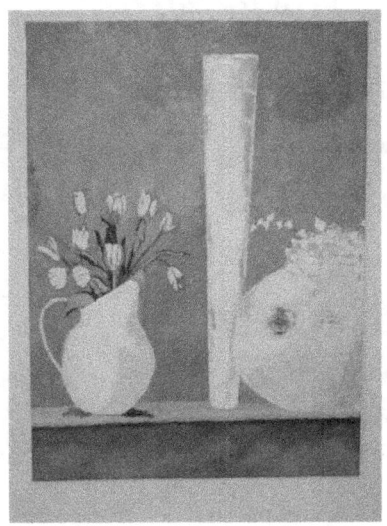

AFRICIAN ART 2013

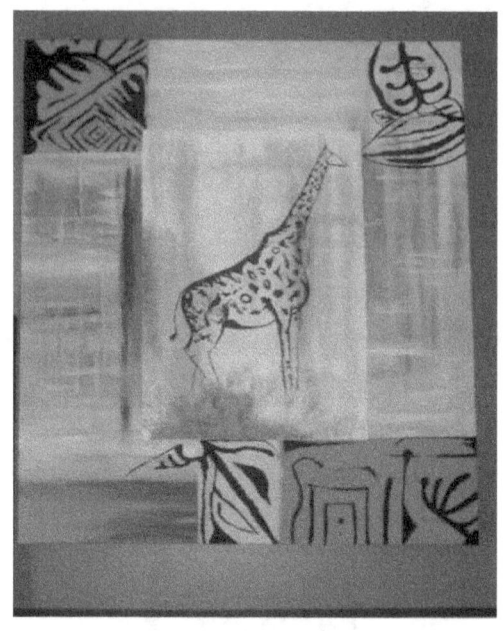

POWER 2013

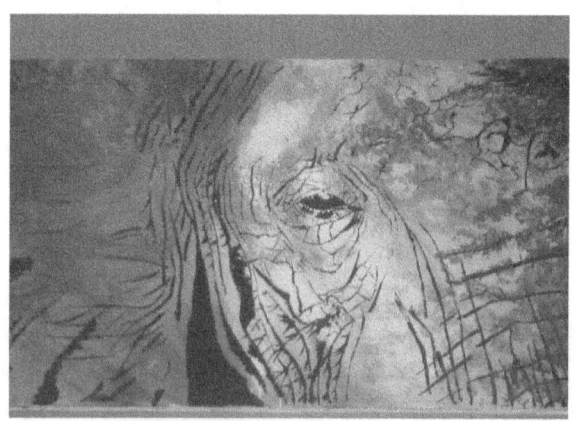

GO EAGLES 2011

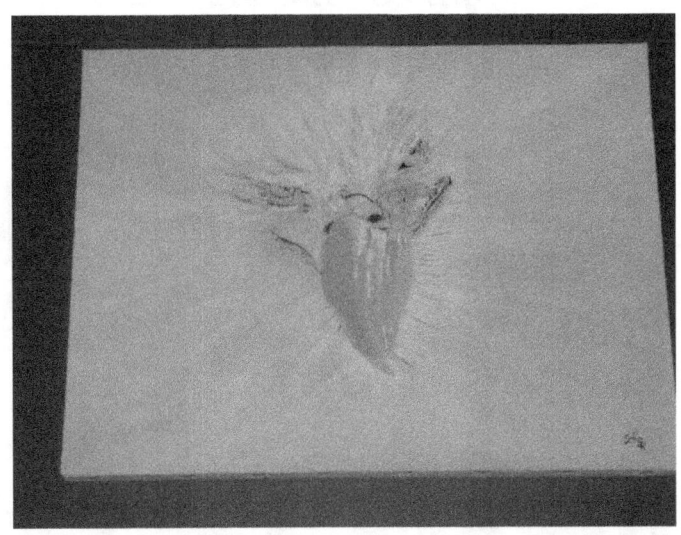

SILVER FOX 2013

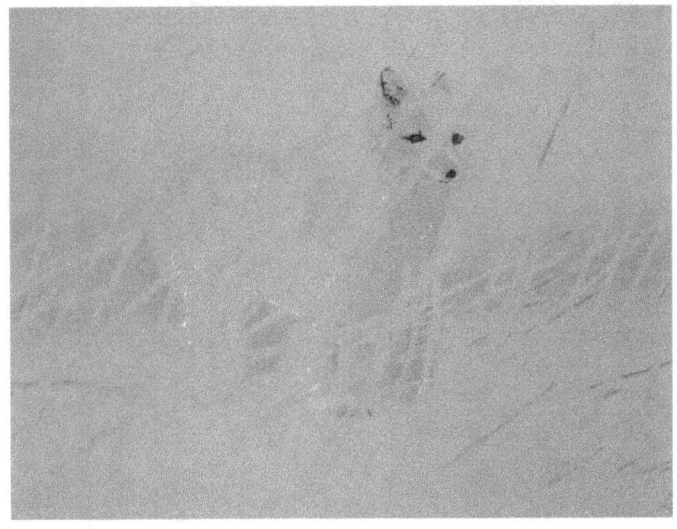

PURE POWER 2012

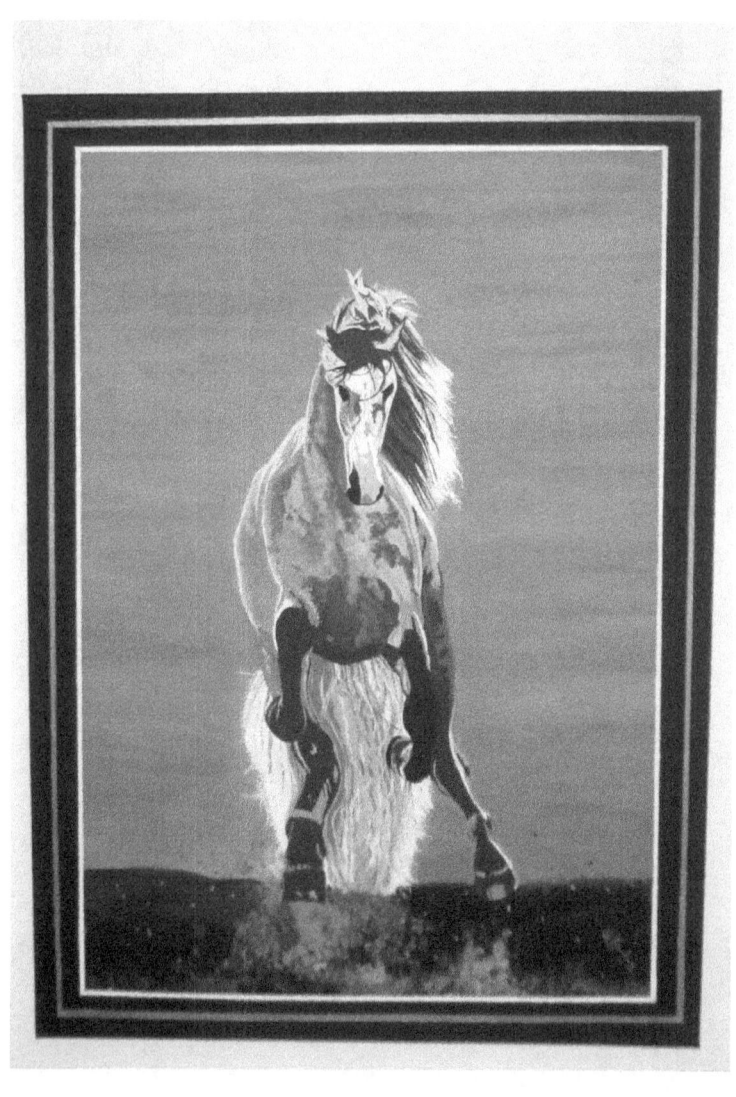

RED ZEBRA 2013

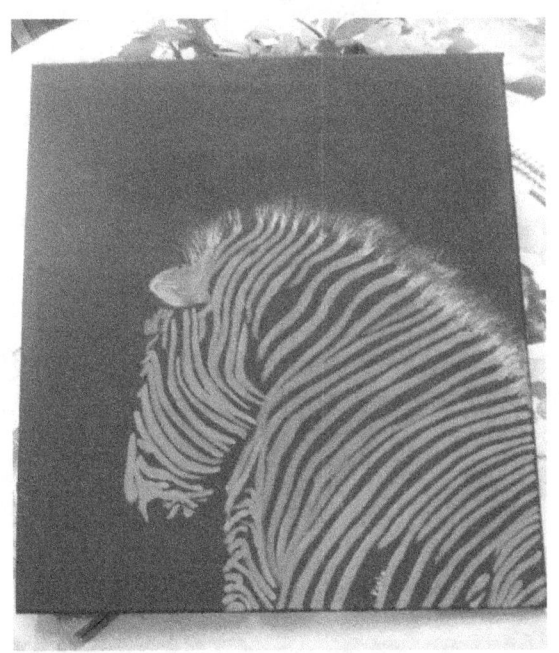

PREATY BUTERFLY 2013

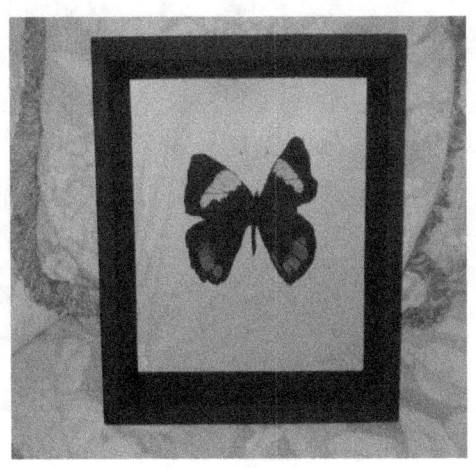

SUNSET HORSES 2013

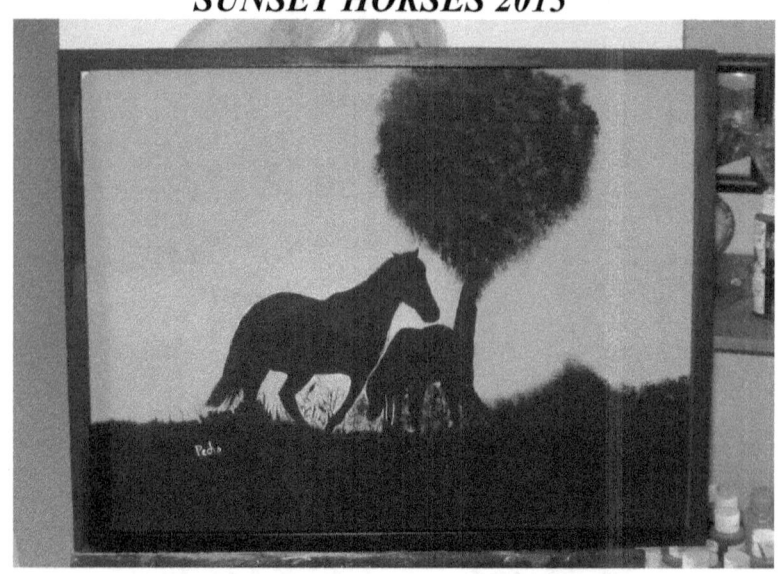

HORSE LOVE 2013

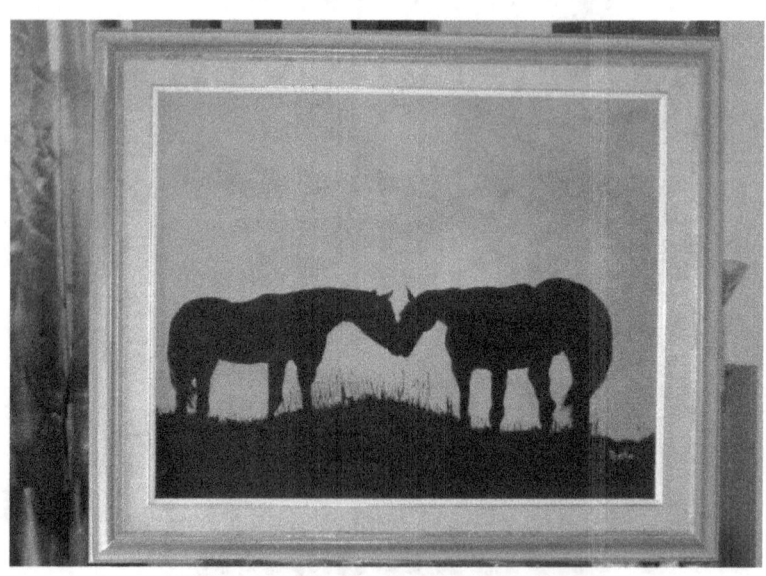

CIRCLES 2012

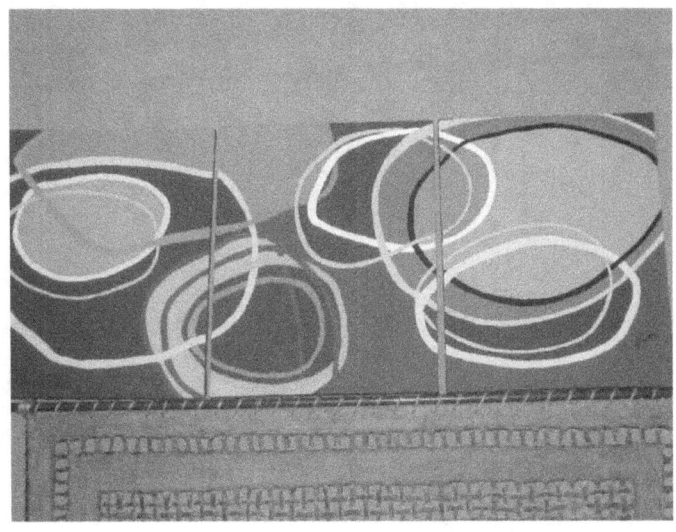

HOWLING 2013

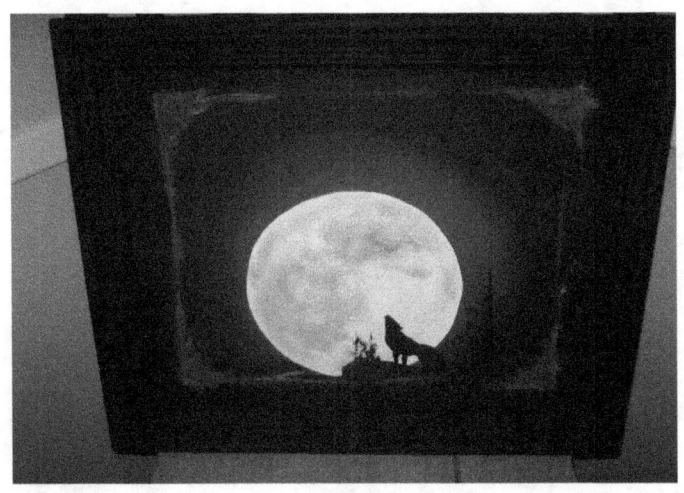

STRONG AND POWERFUL 2013

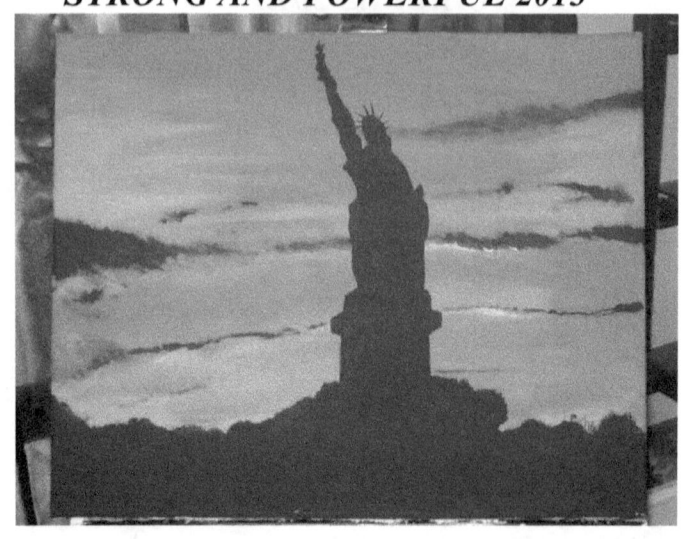

OUR LADY 2013

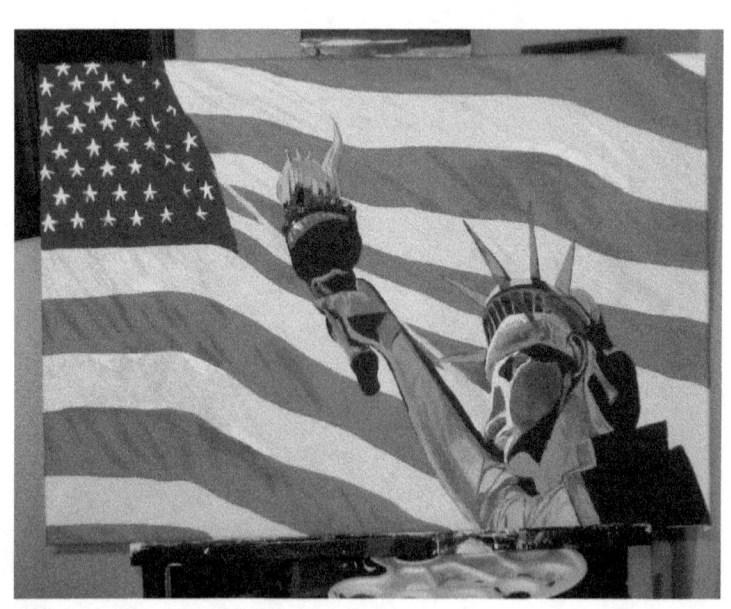

COFFEE TIME 2011

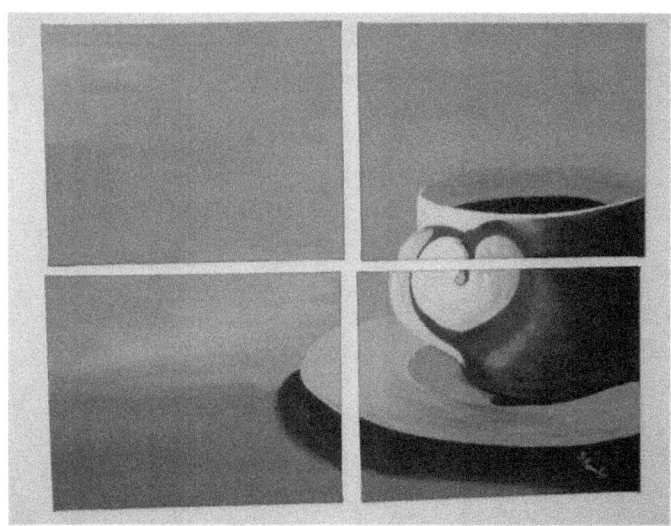

POWERFUL LADY 2013

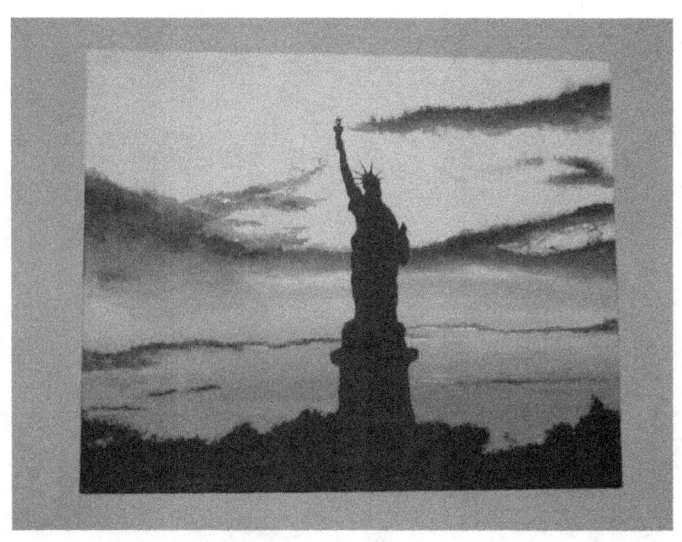

ALIEN FLOWERS IN BLOOM 2013

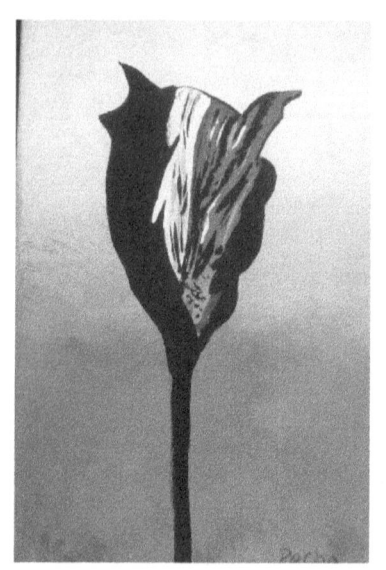 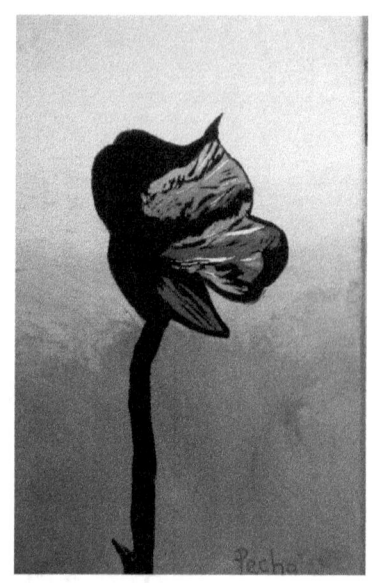

TABLE IN PARIS 2013

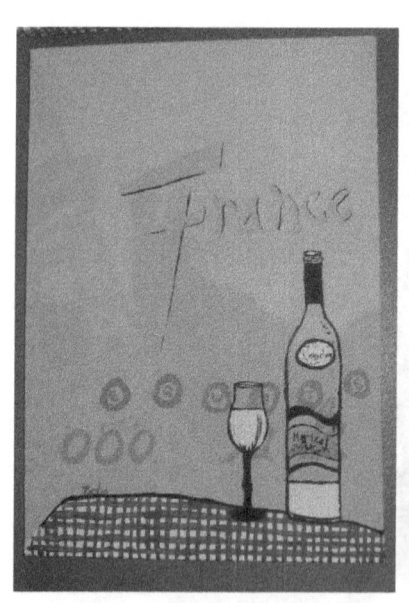 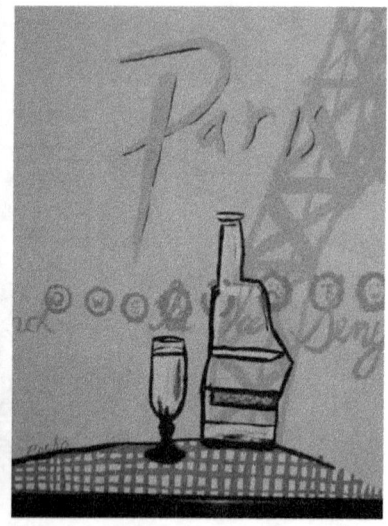

NIAGARA TABLE 2012

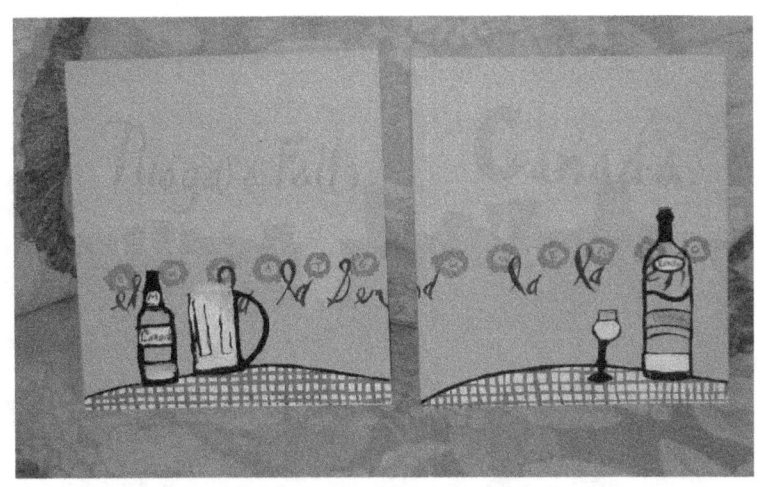

MOUNT RUSHMORE 2013

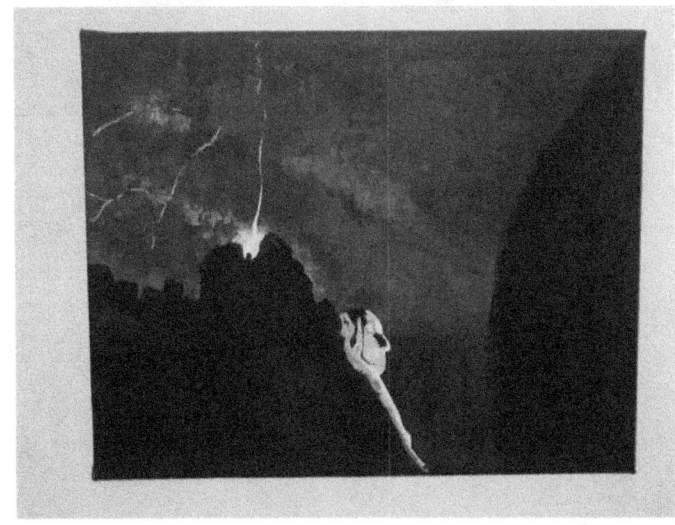

TWO SIDES OD VIEW 2013

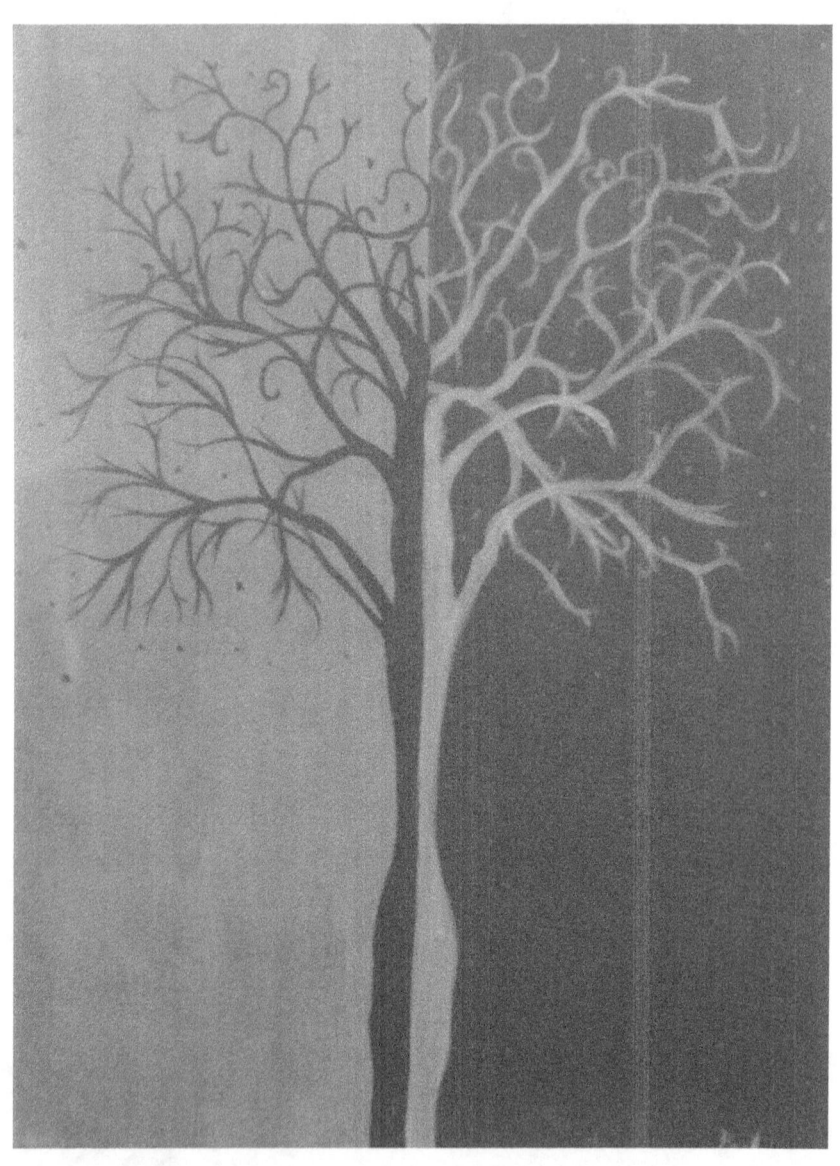

THE WOODS 2014

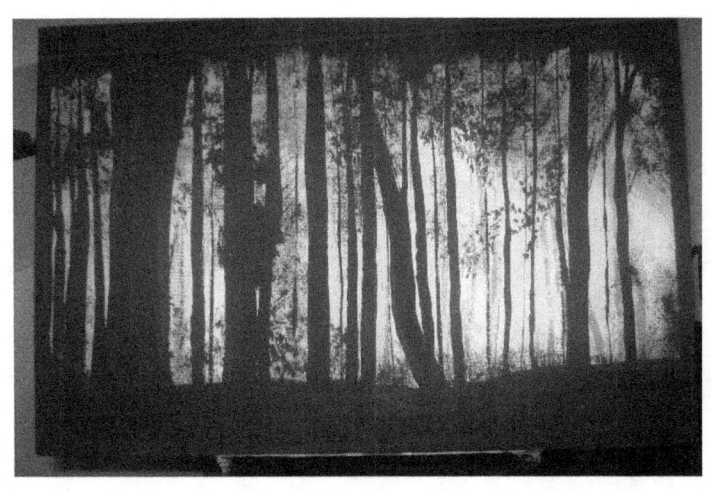

LOVE 2012

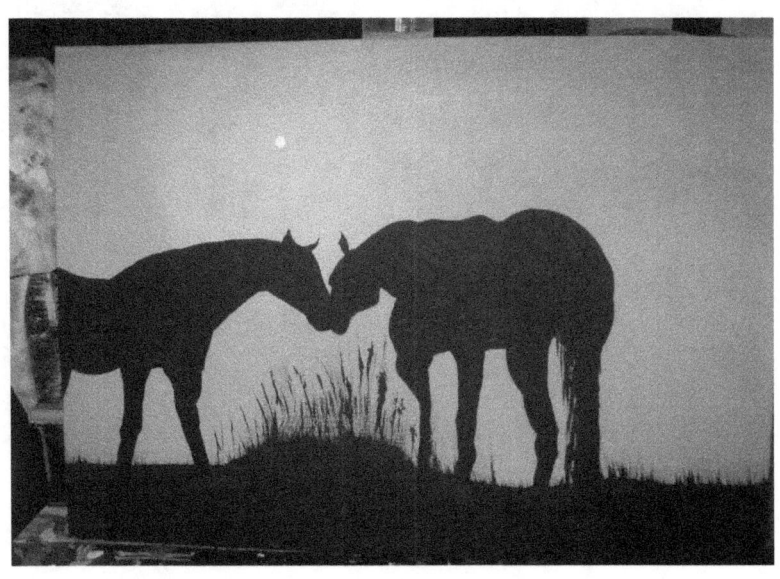

LIFE AFTER DEATH 2013

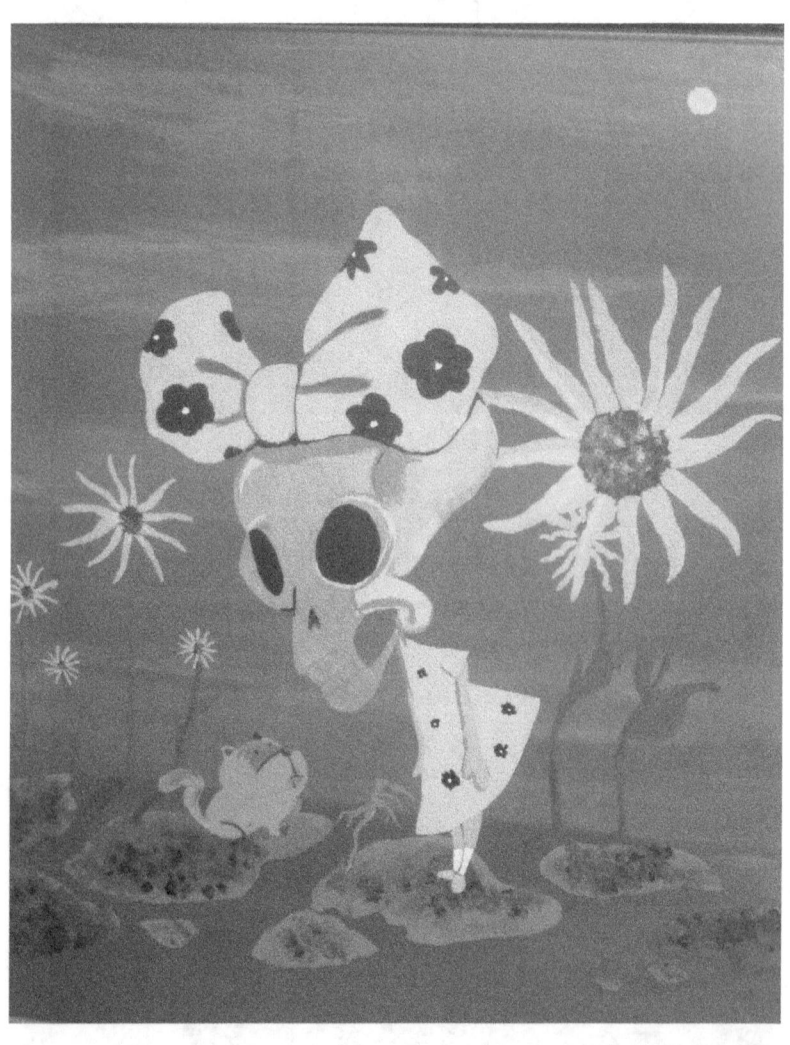

THE KEYHOLE 2014

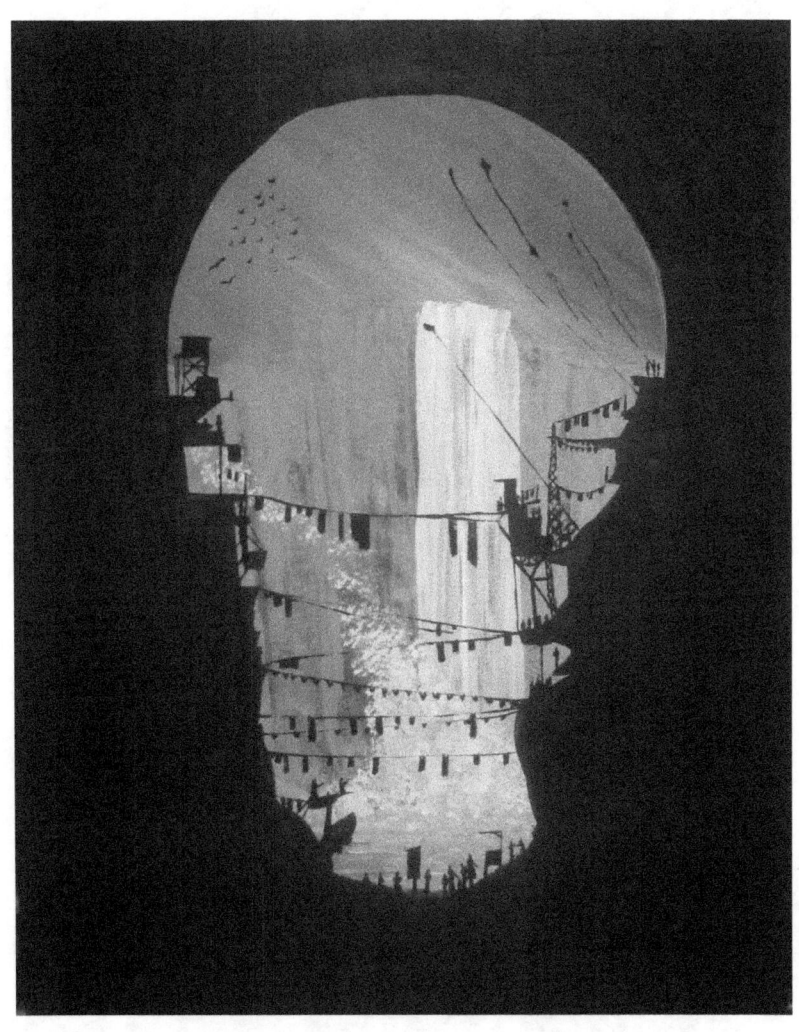

SAILING AWAY 2013

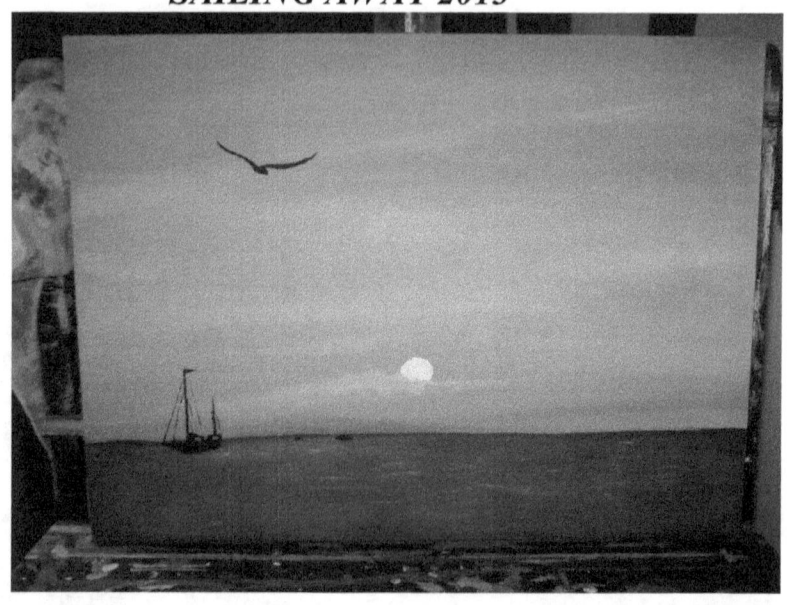

SUNSET IN LOVE 2014

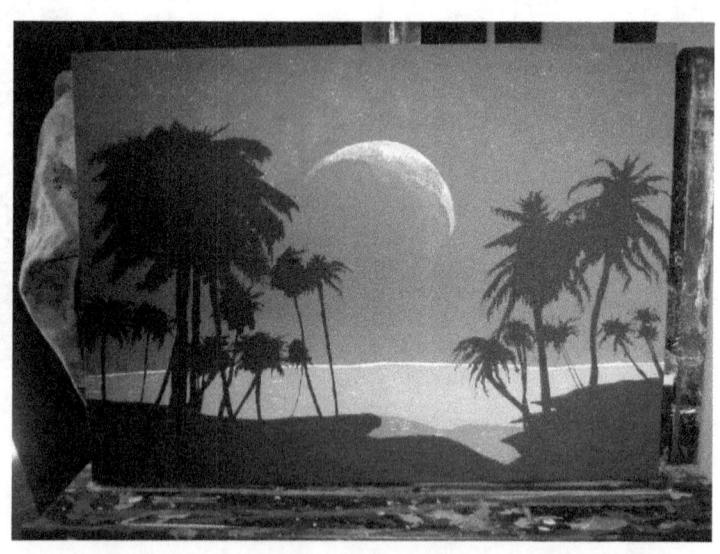

WINTER COLD 2013

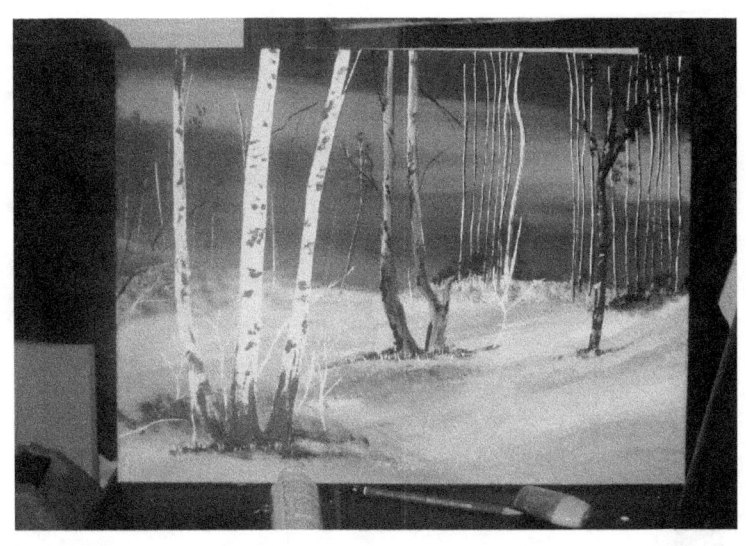

THE COLD 2013

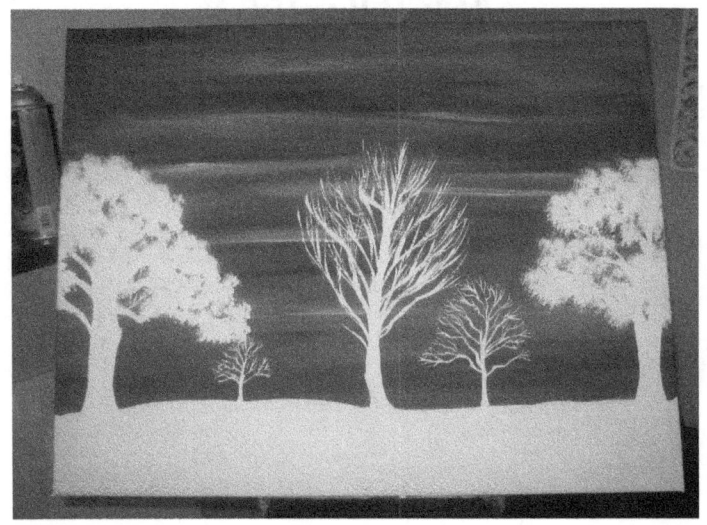

PEGGY'S BRIDGE 2012

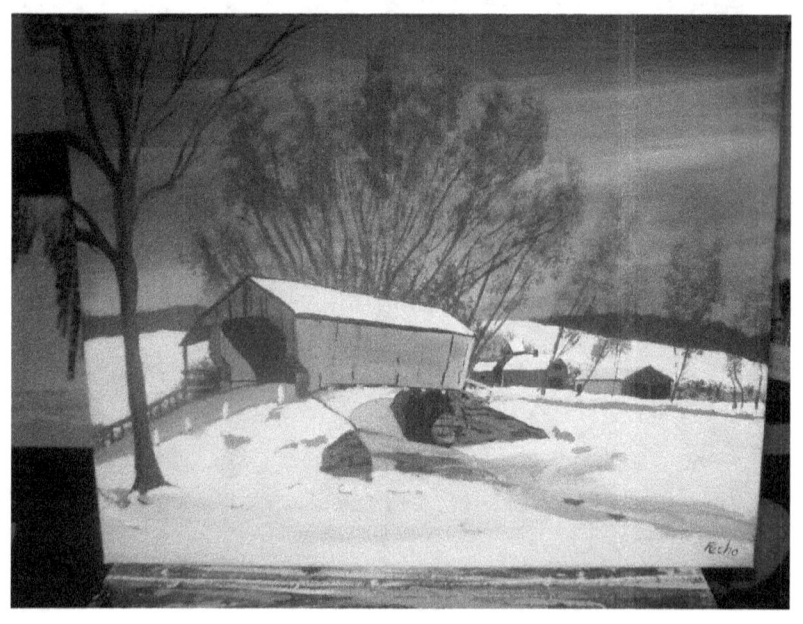

BIRCH WOODS 2013

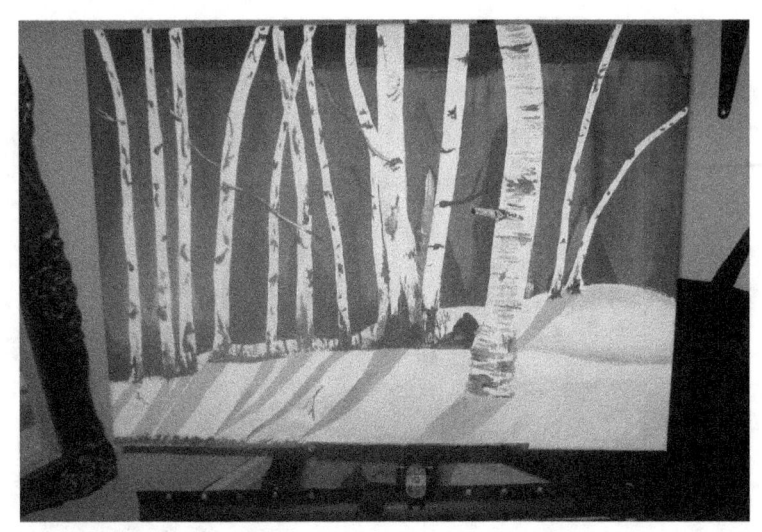

WINTER STORM 2013

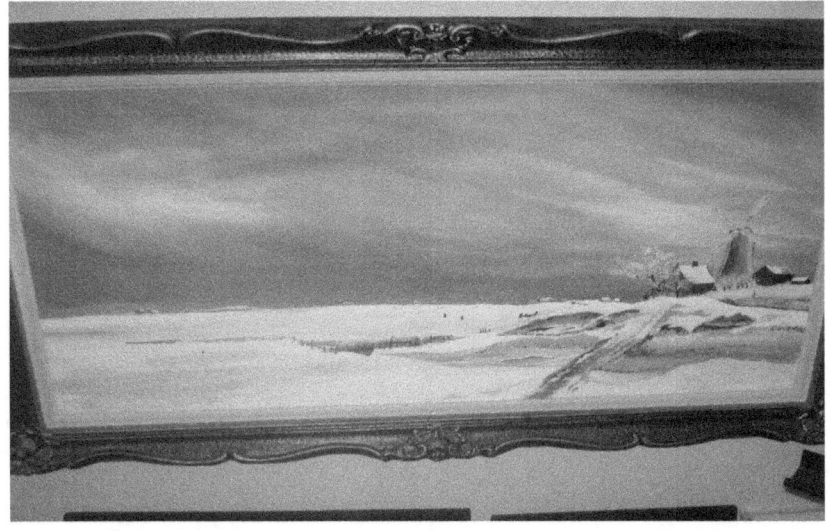

THE OL FARM 2013

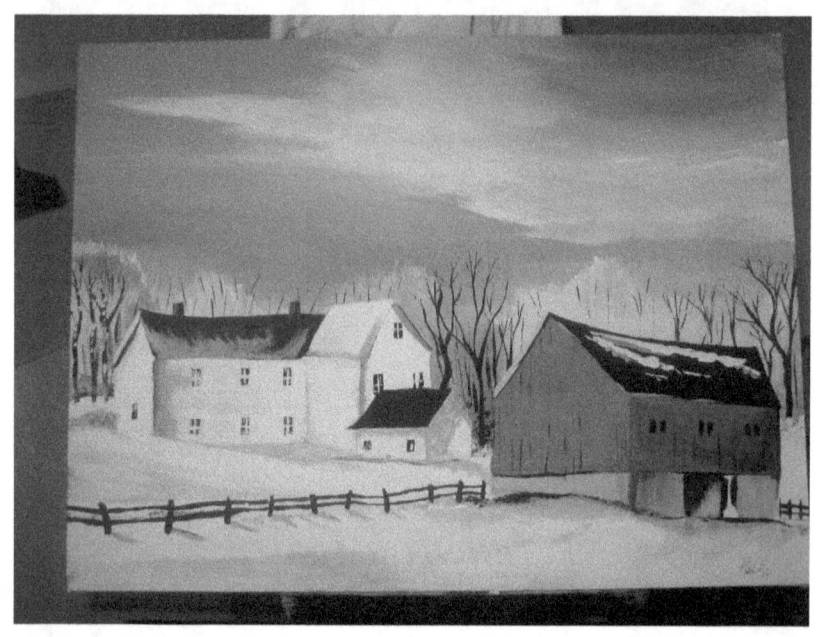

FANTASY WINTER 2014

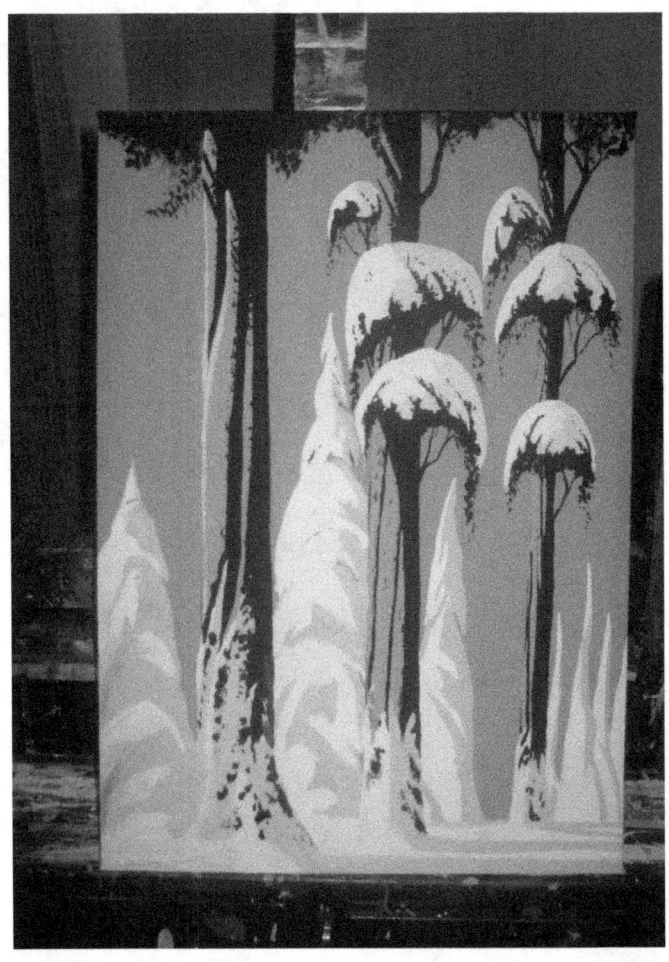

THE FARM 2014

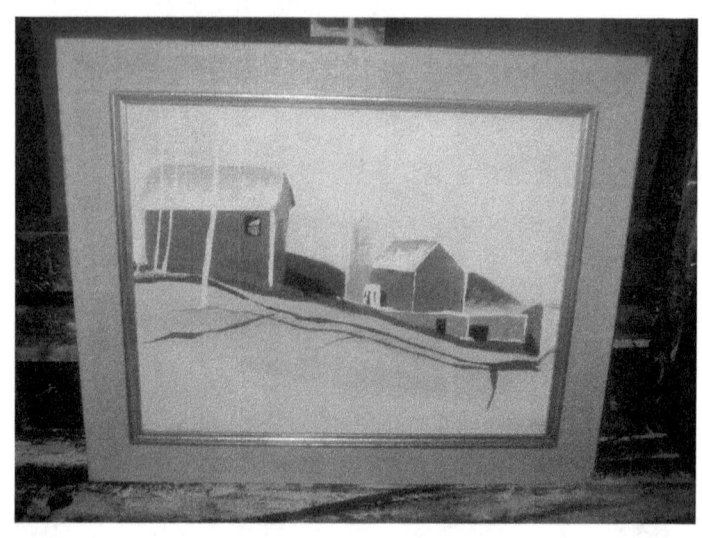

NIAGARA FALLS 2014

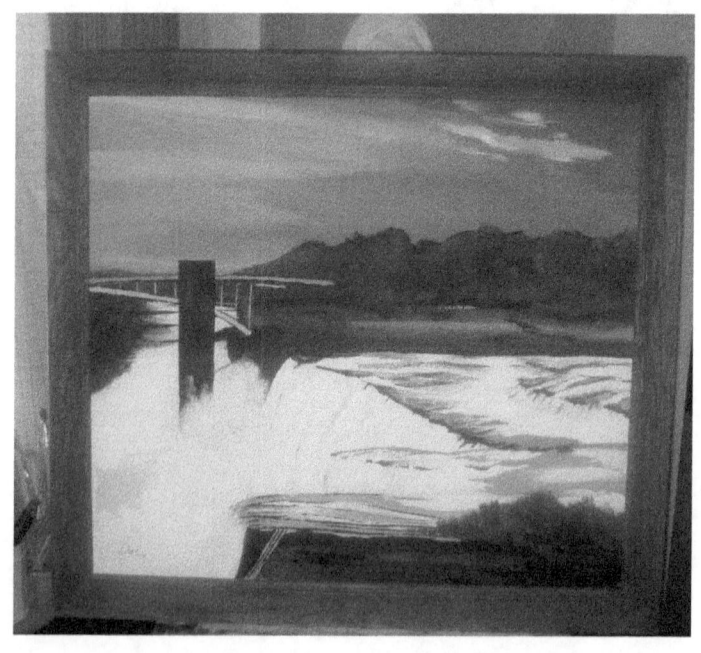

NIAGARA FALLS 2013

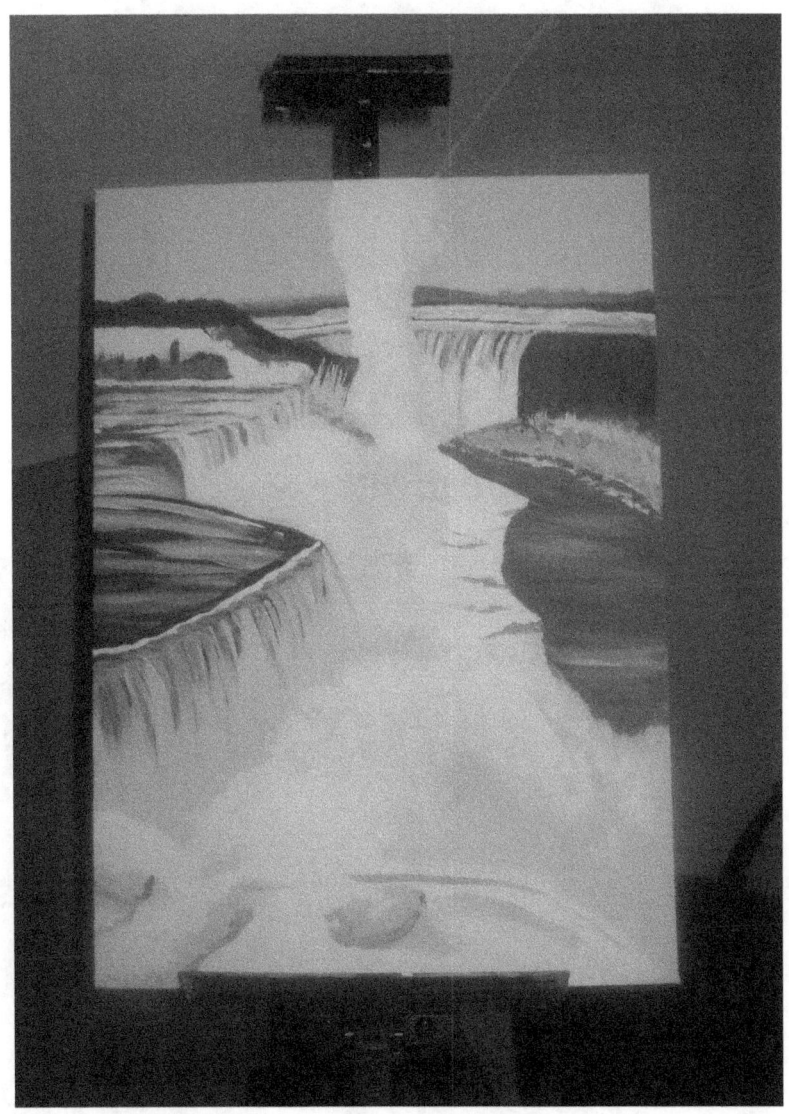

THE GREAT HORSESHOE FALLS 2014

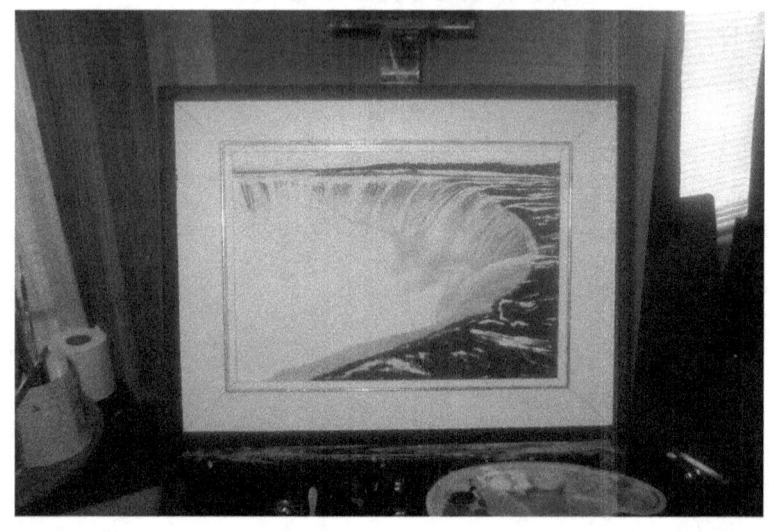

BLOOM 2014

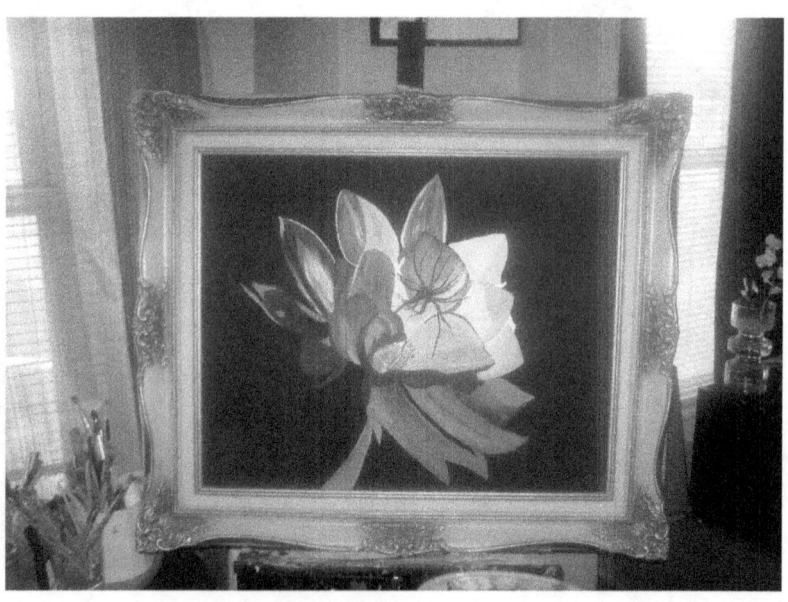

WINTER 2014

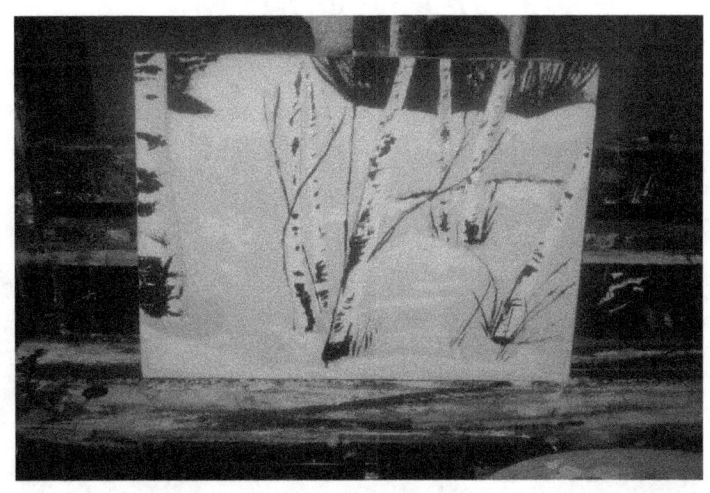

NIAGARA MIST 2014

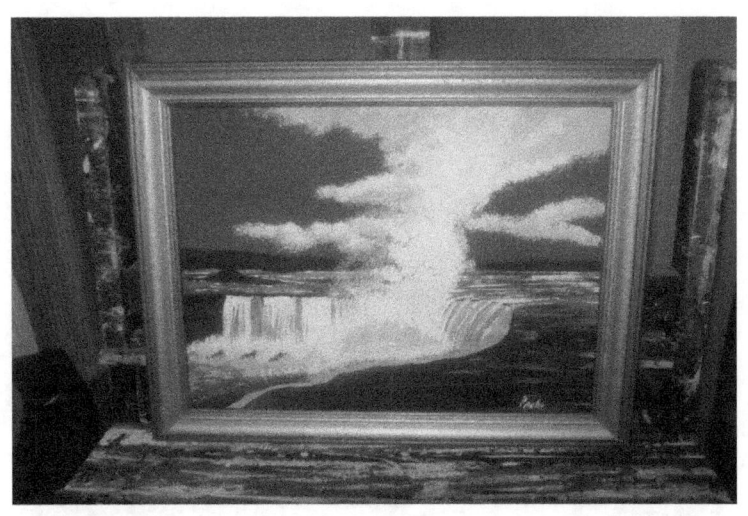

NIAGARA AT NIGHT 2014

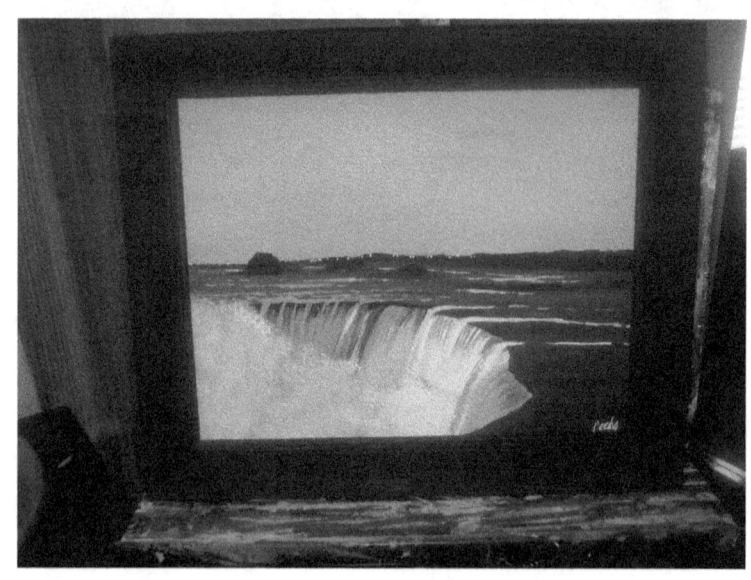

THE FALLS 2014

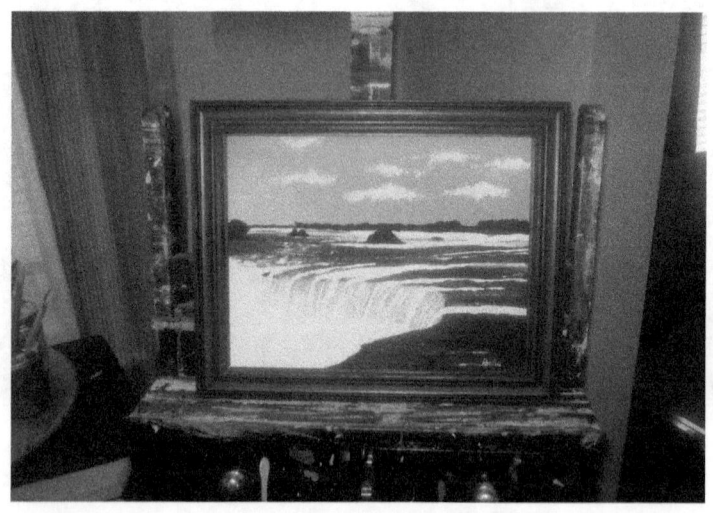

ELEPHANTS 2014

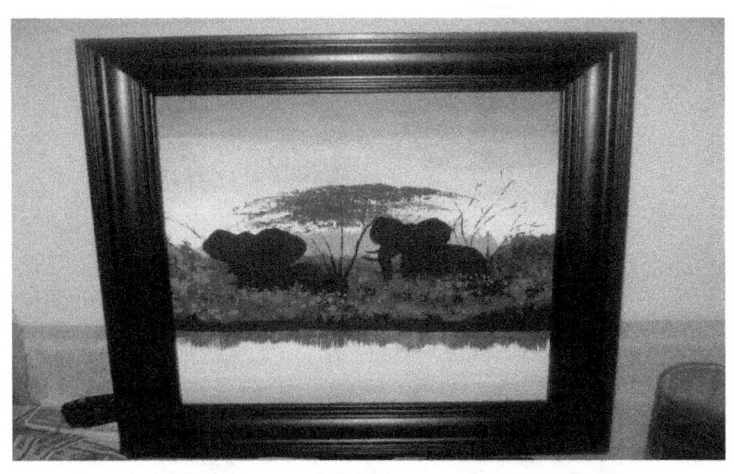

THE WOODS 2014

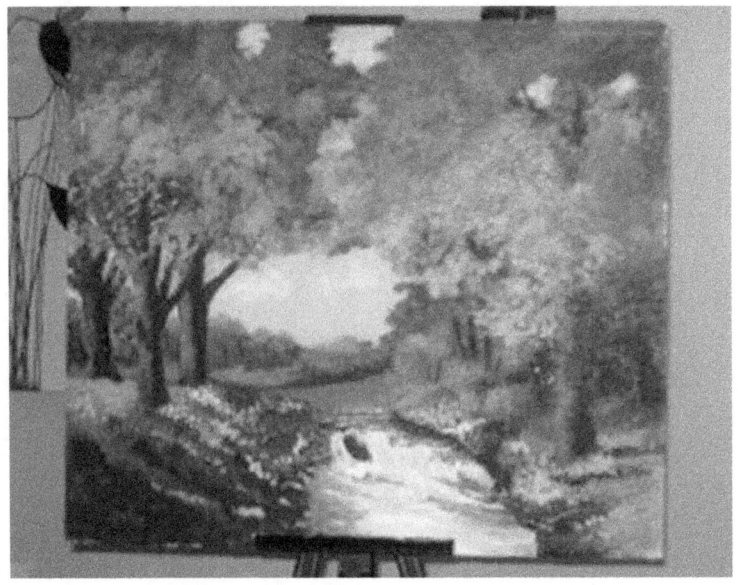

AFRICA LAND 2014

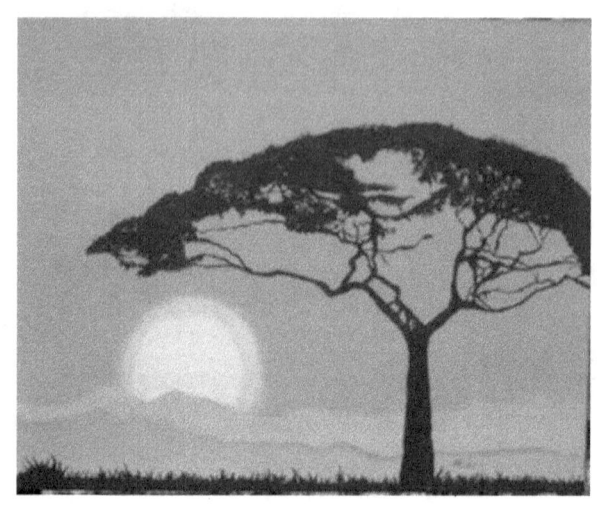

SERENITY 2014

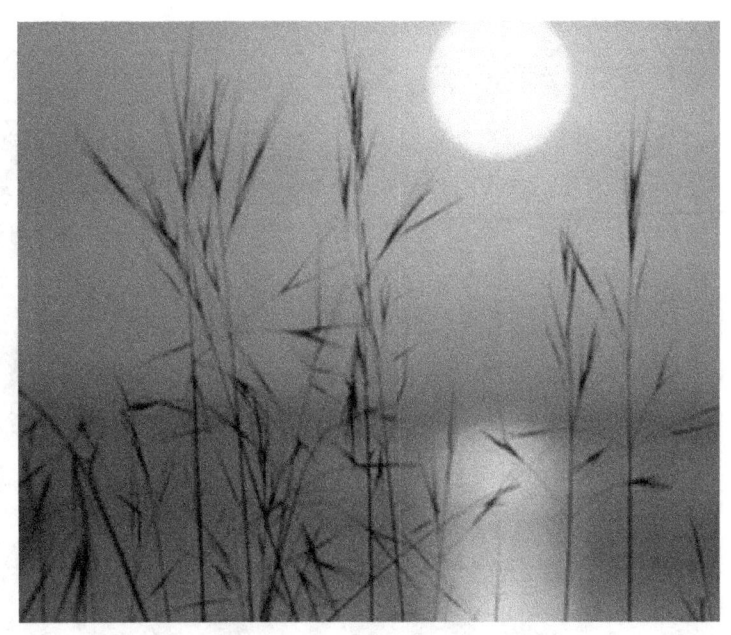

RAINBOW LAND 2013

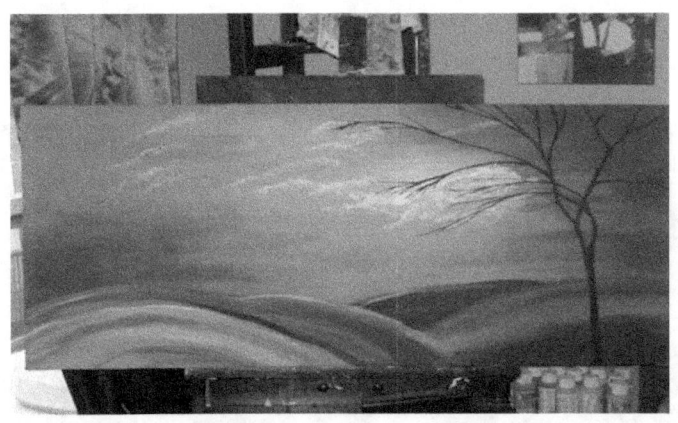

SAILING AWAY 2014

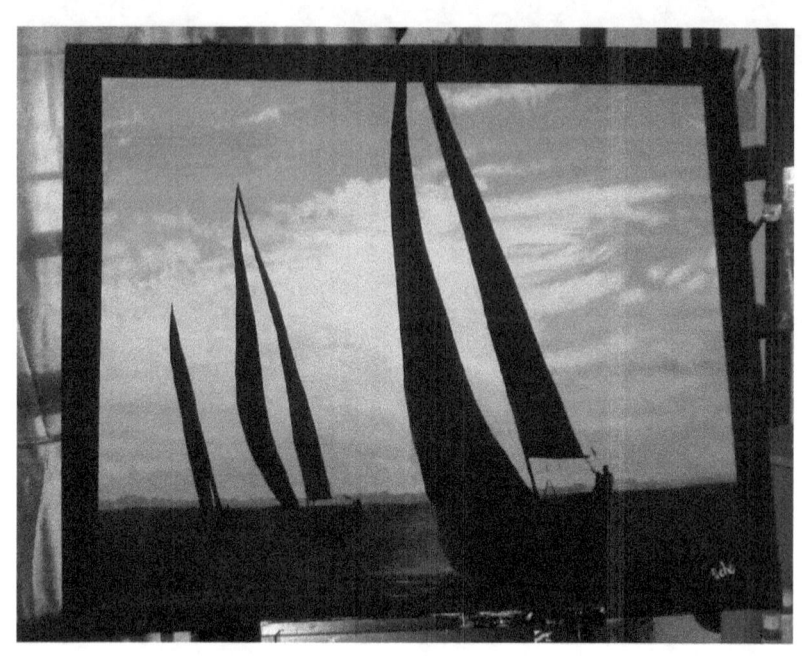

WAVES 2013

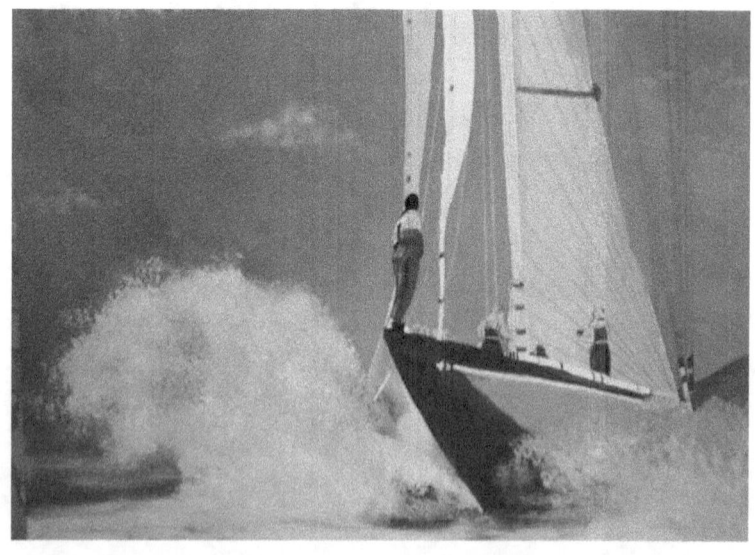

HMSC MCKENNZIE 2013

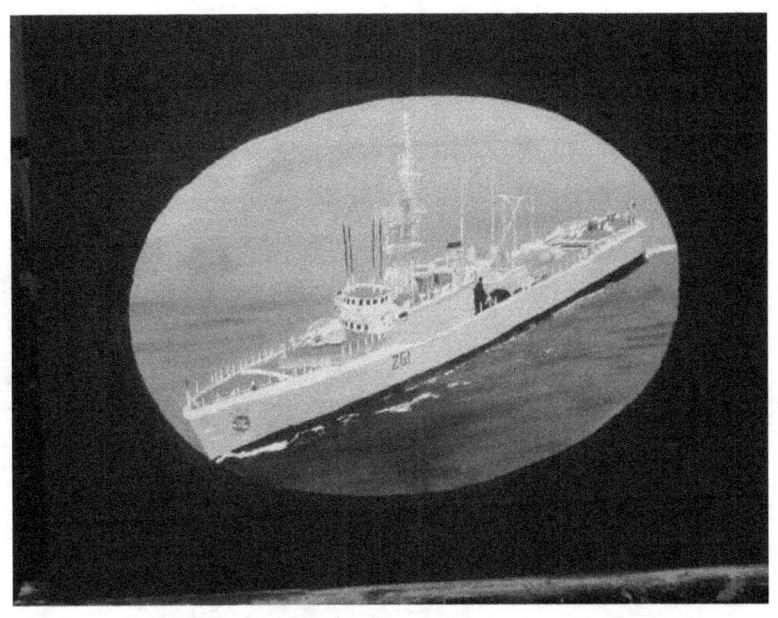

PECHO 2013

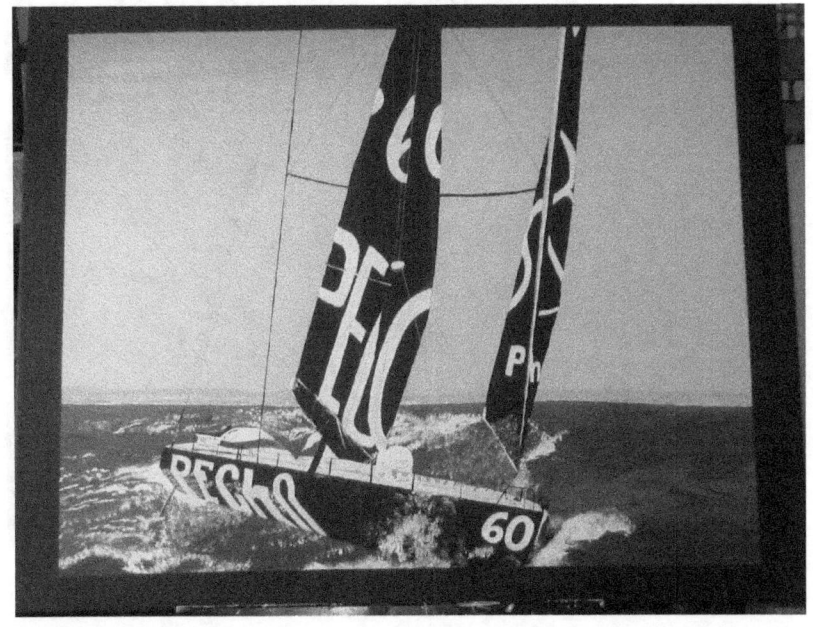

TALL SHIP 2013

BATMAN 2013

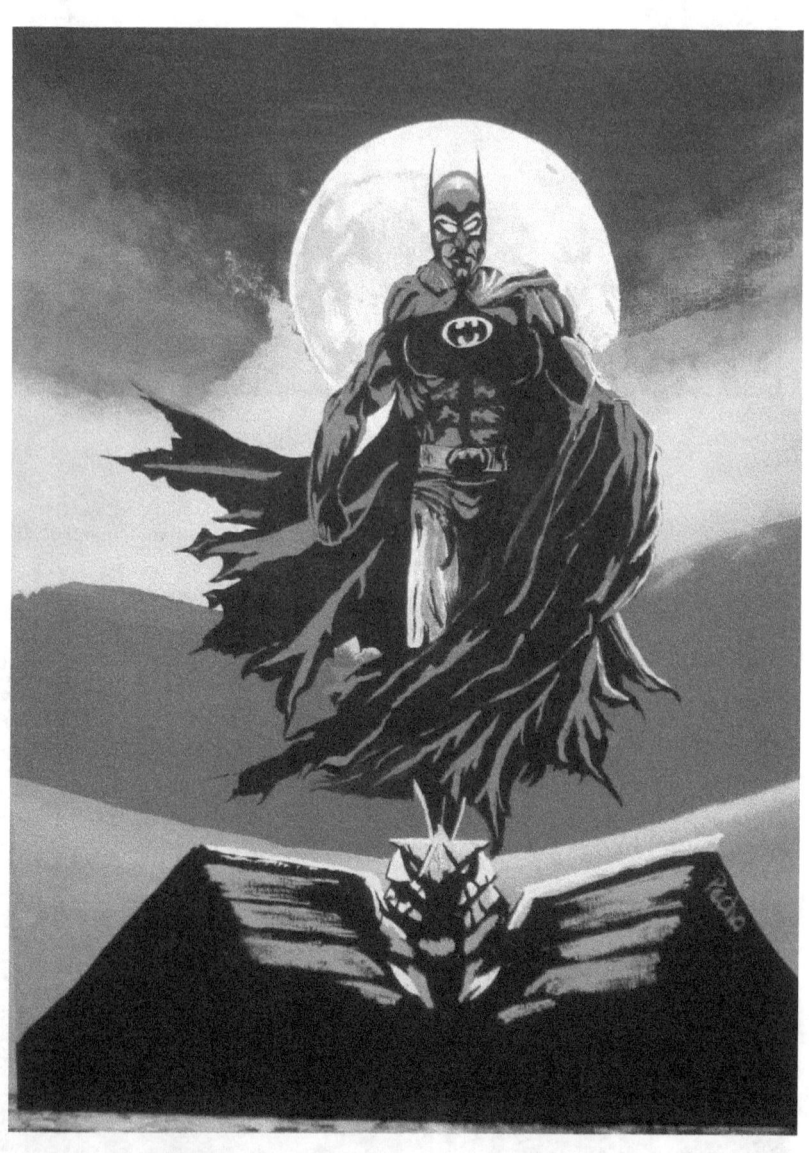

CAPTAIN AMERICA 2013

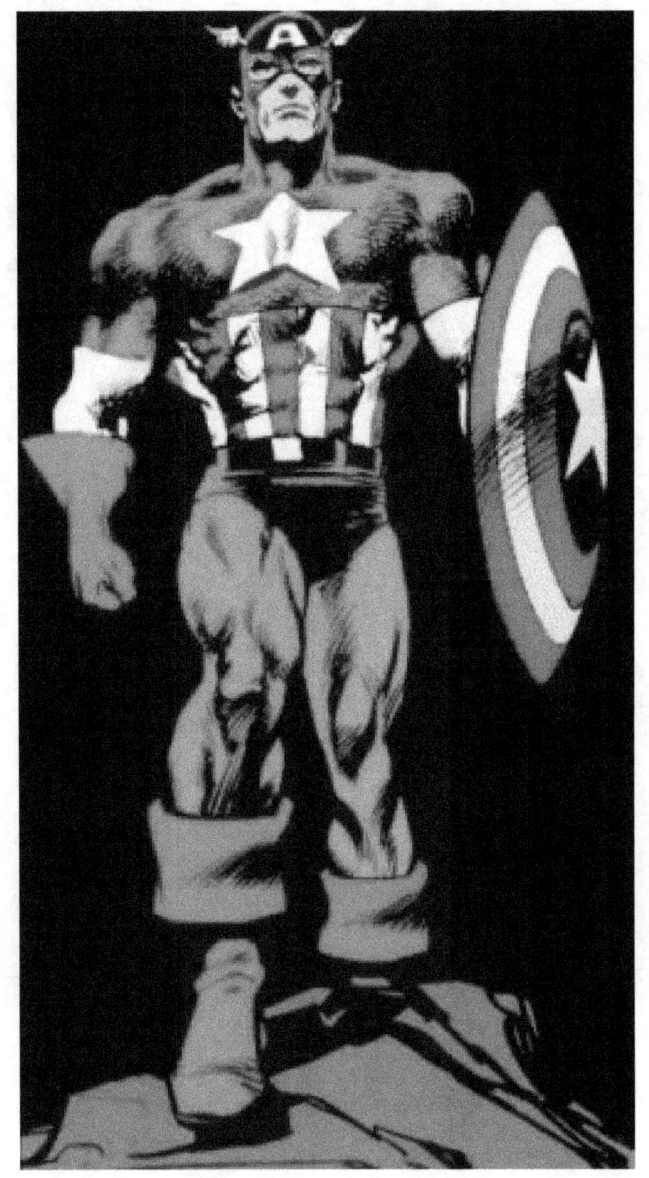

FRANKENSTIEN 2012

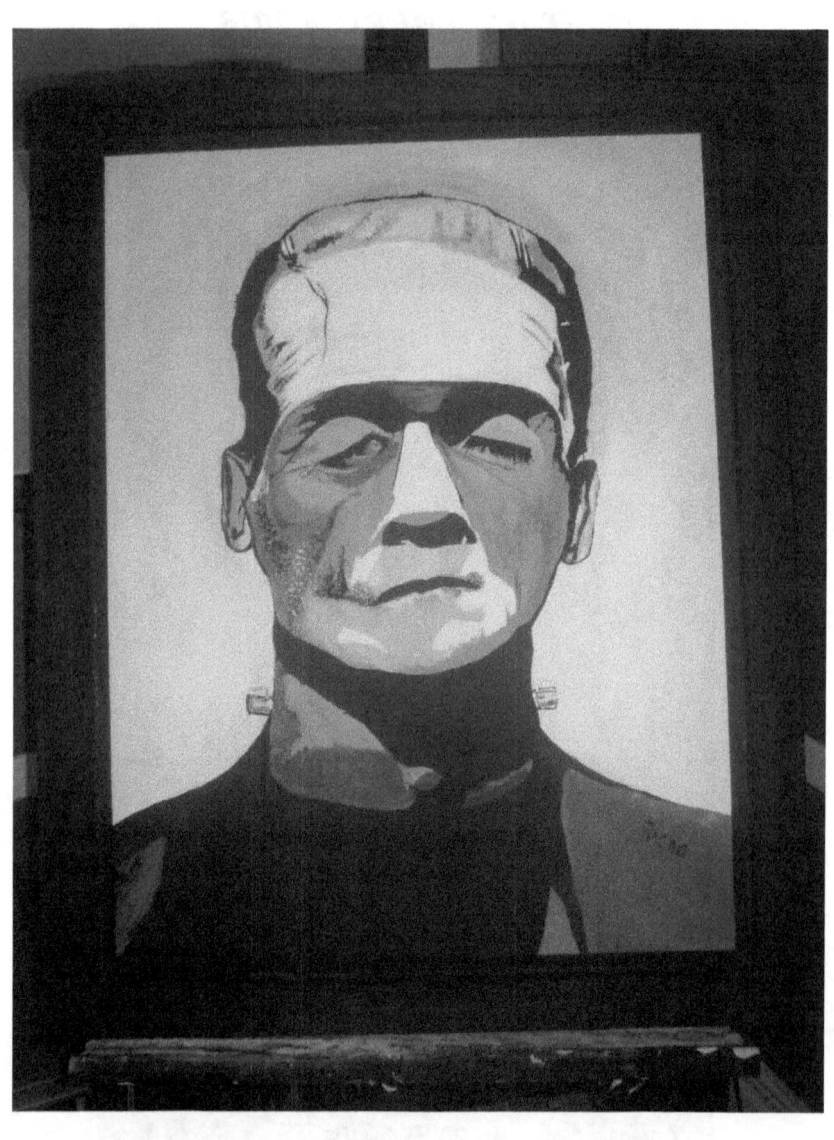

VENIM 2013

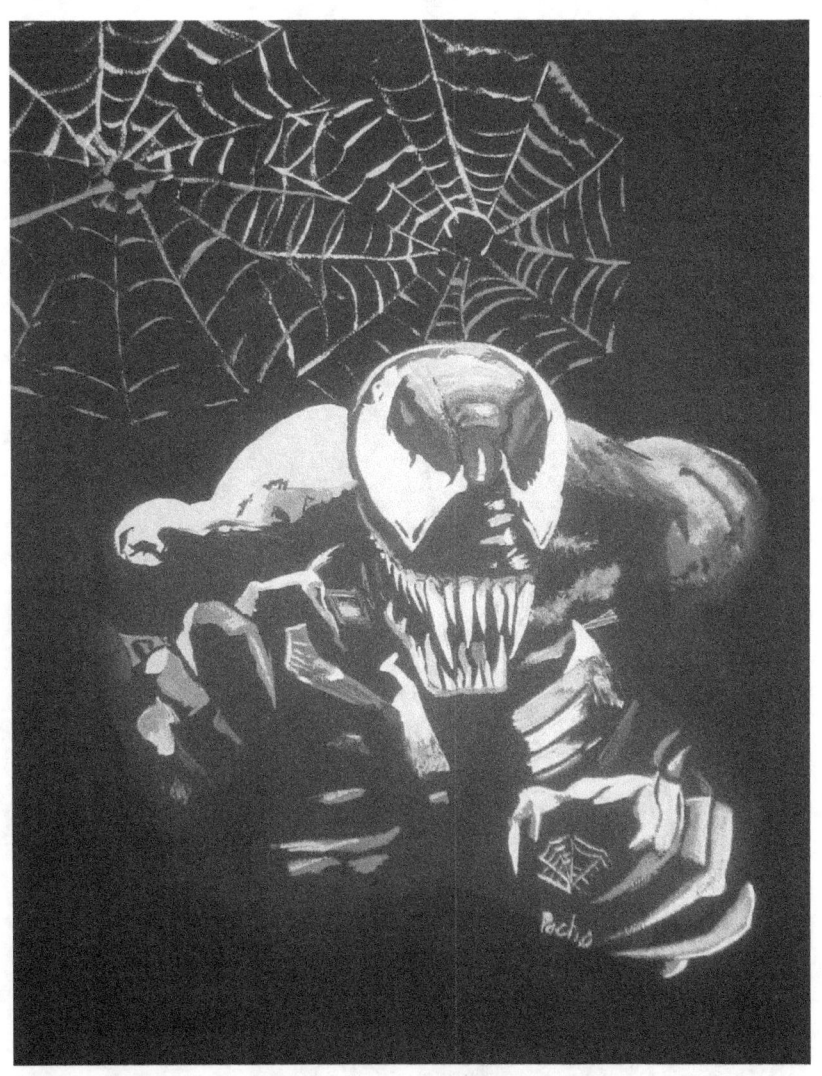

GREEN LANTERN 2013

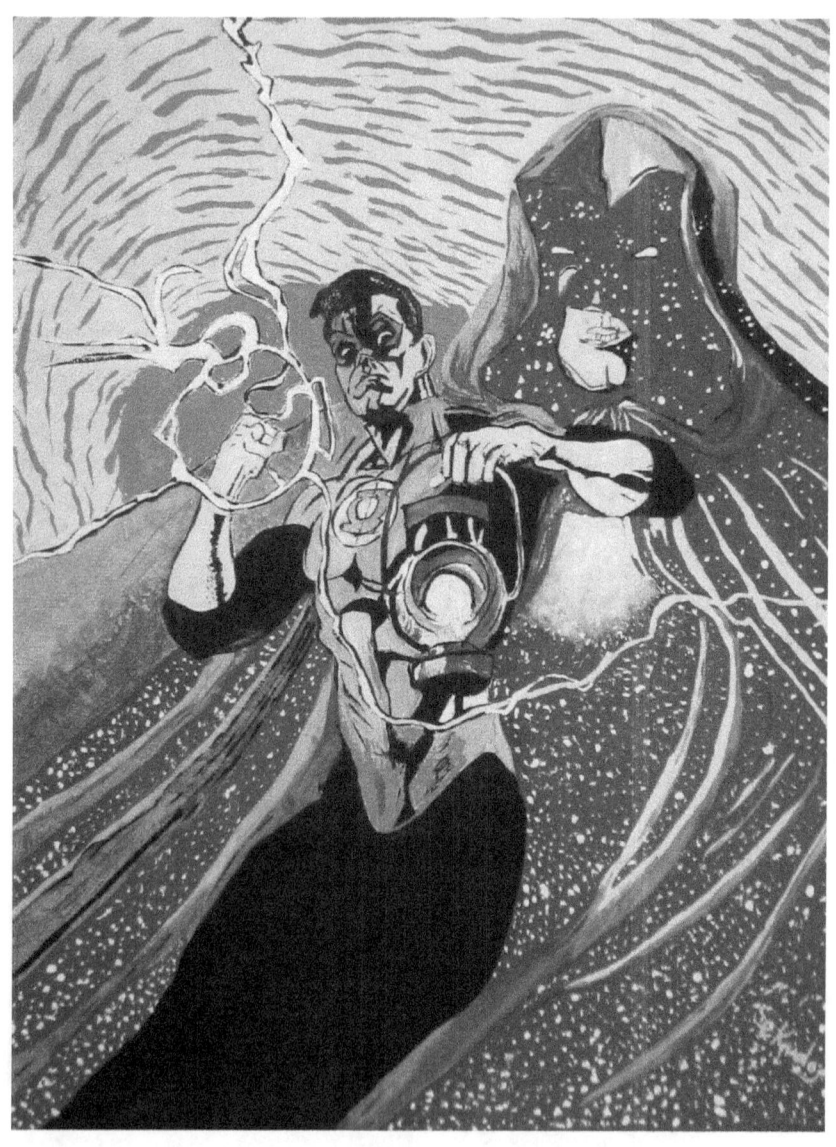

THOR 2013

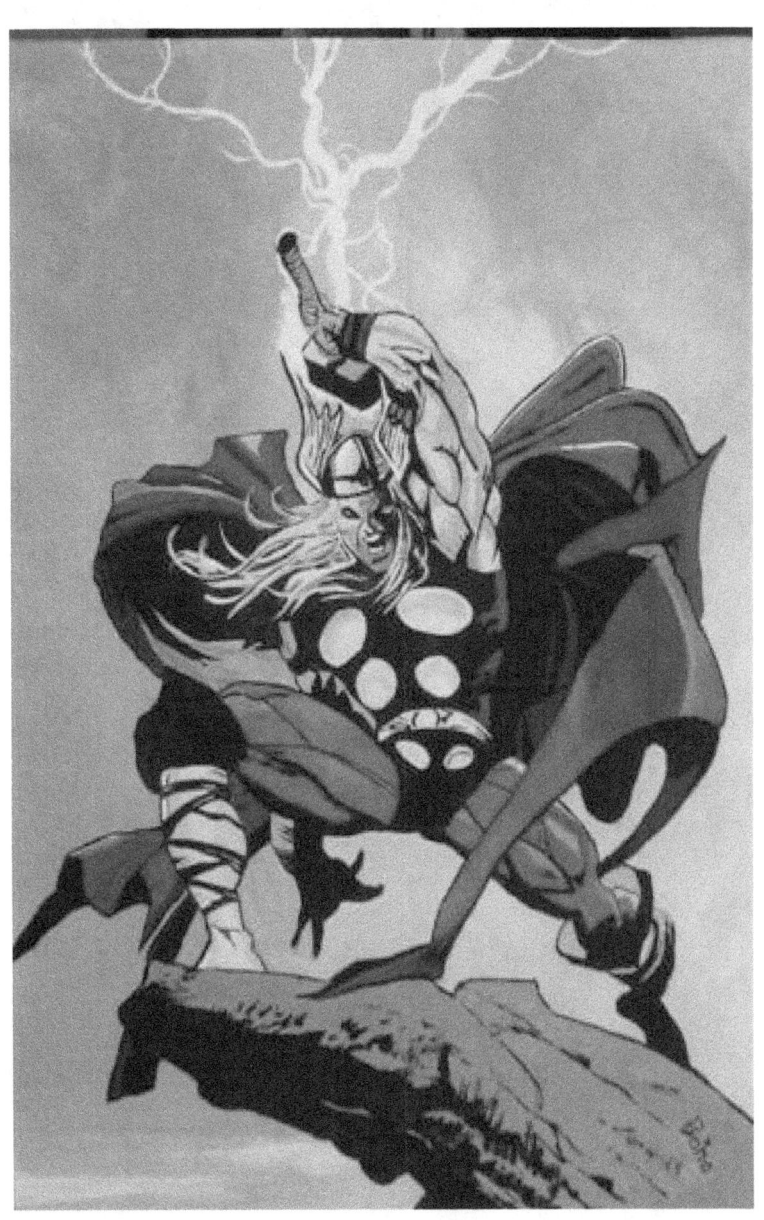

URLOCKER 2013

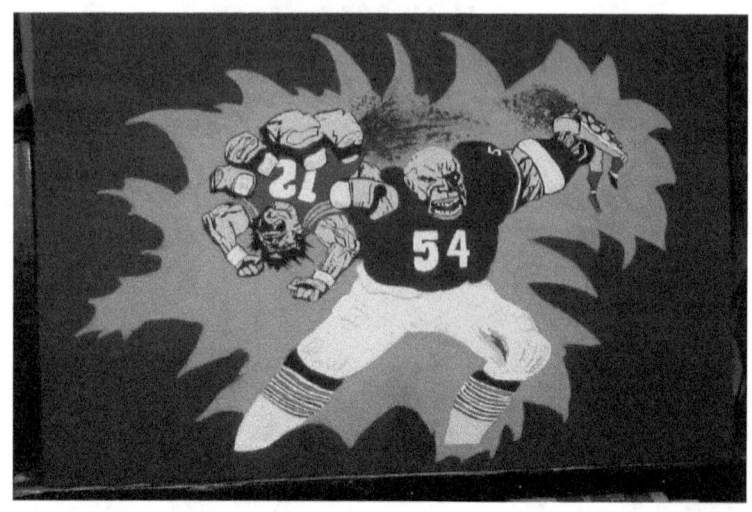

ZORN 2014

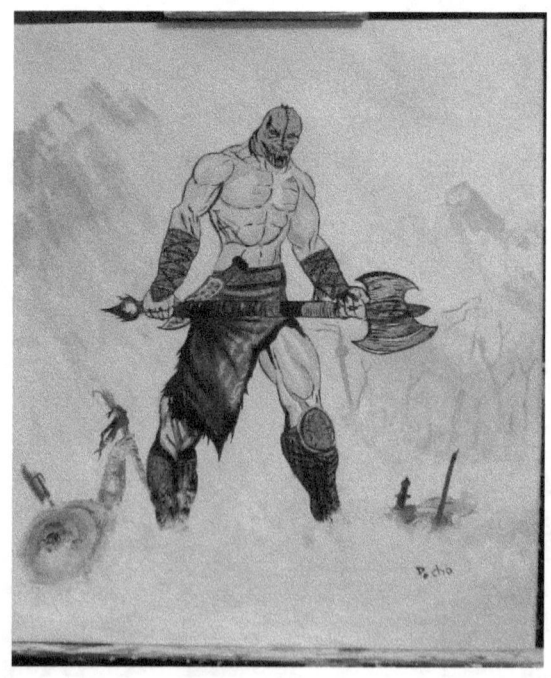

THE STREAM 2013

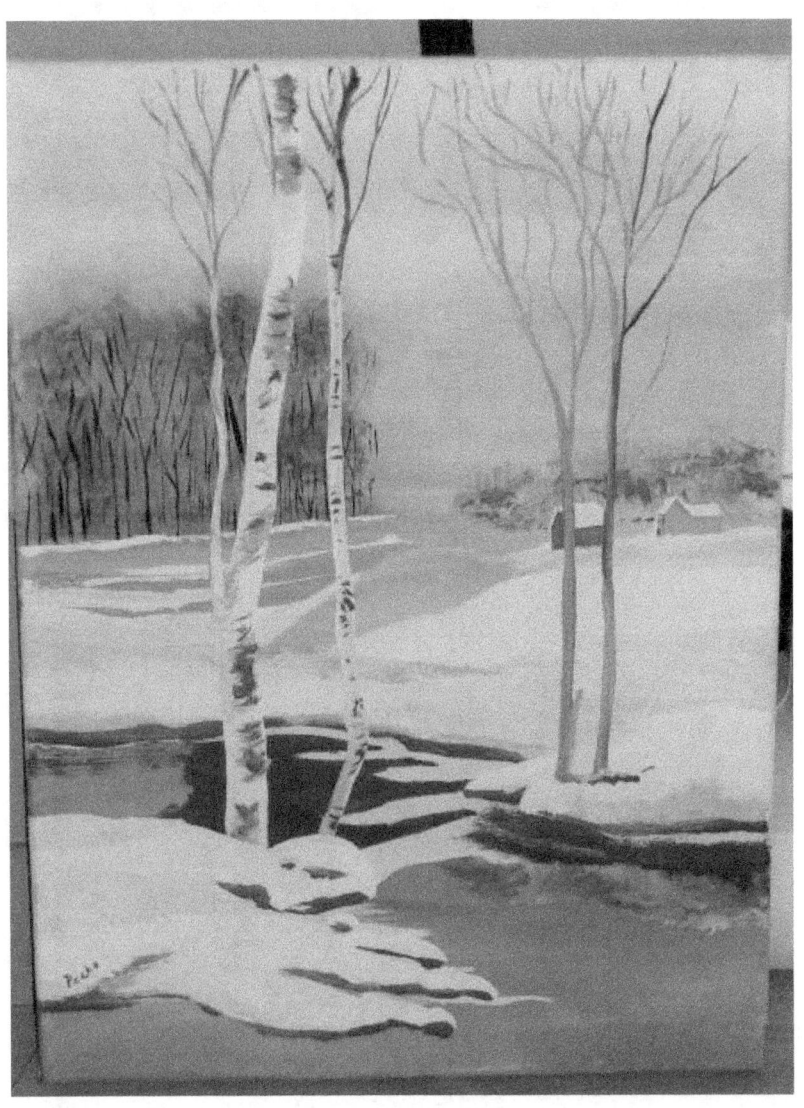

WHEN 2 WORLDS COLIDE 2013

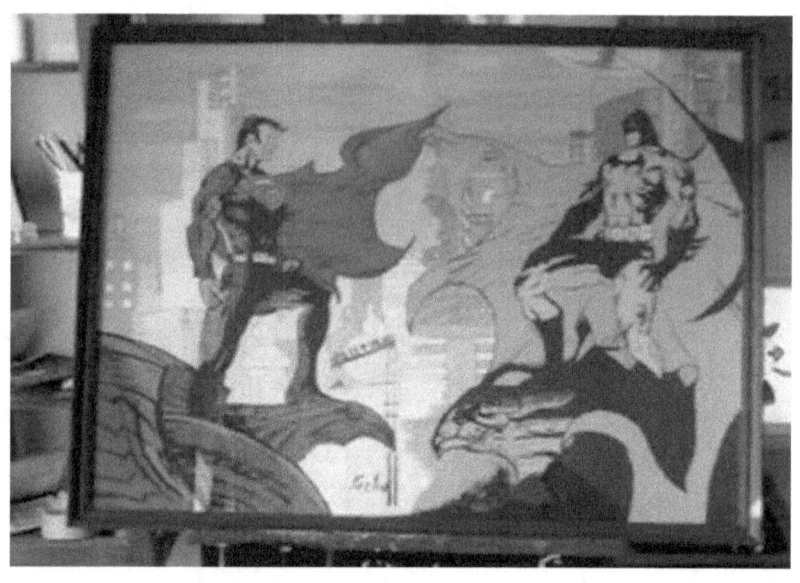

THE PLAINS 2013

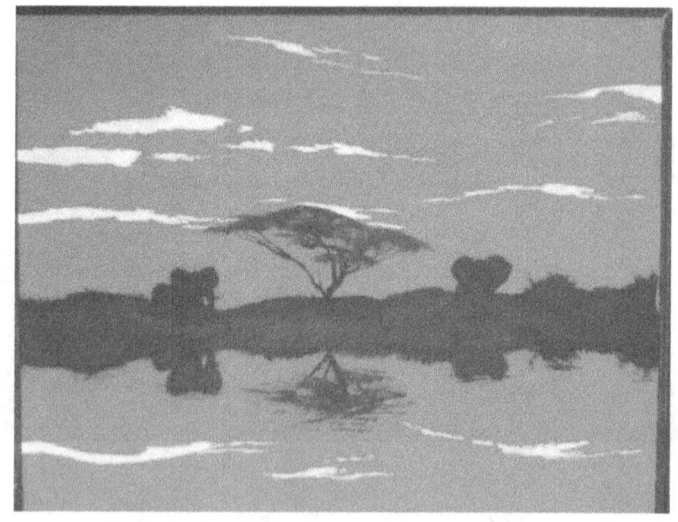

THE ELEPHANT 2014

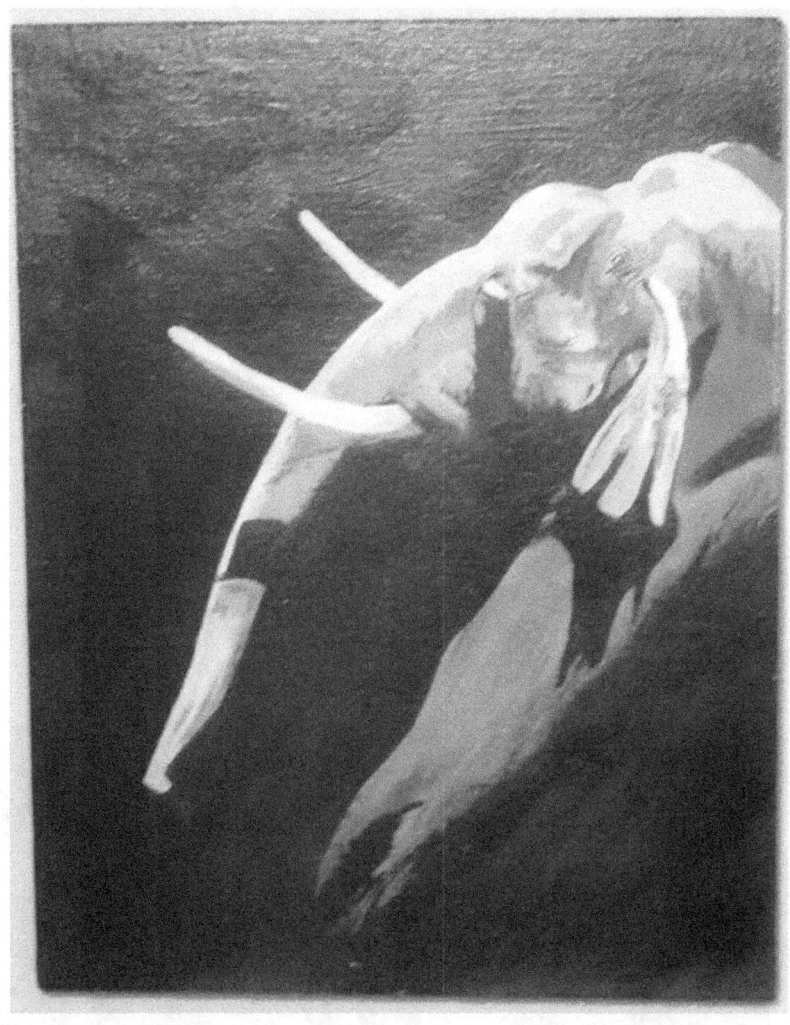

THE FARM 2014

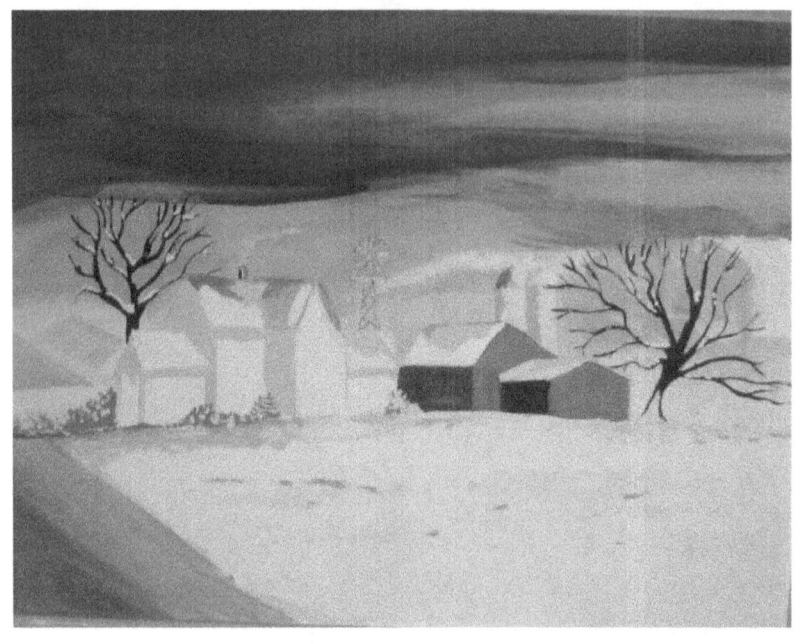

LILLIES 2014

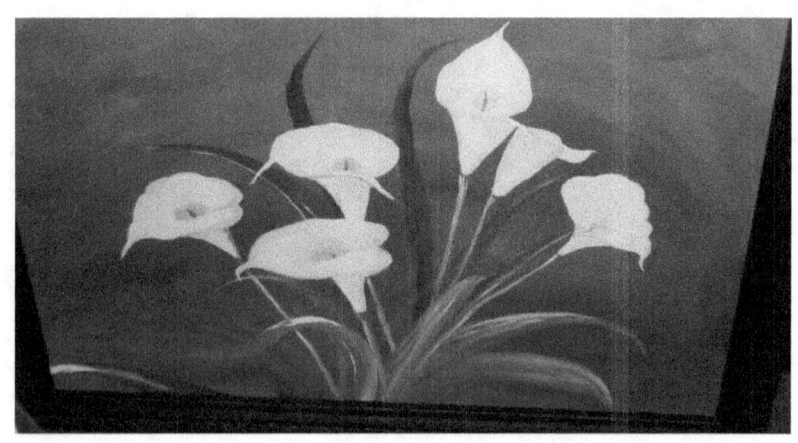

SUNFLOWER 2015

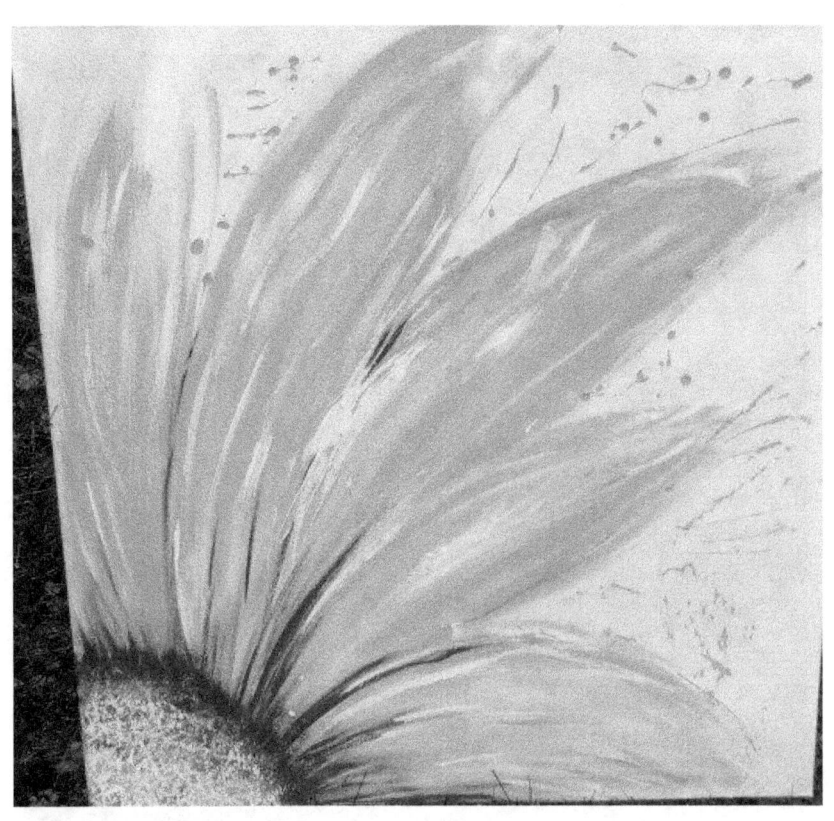

GIRAFFE 2014

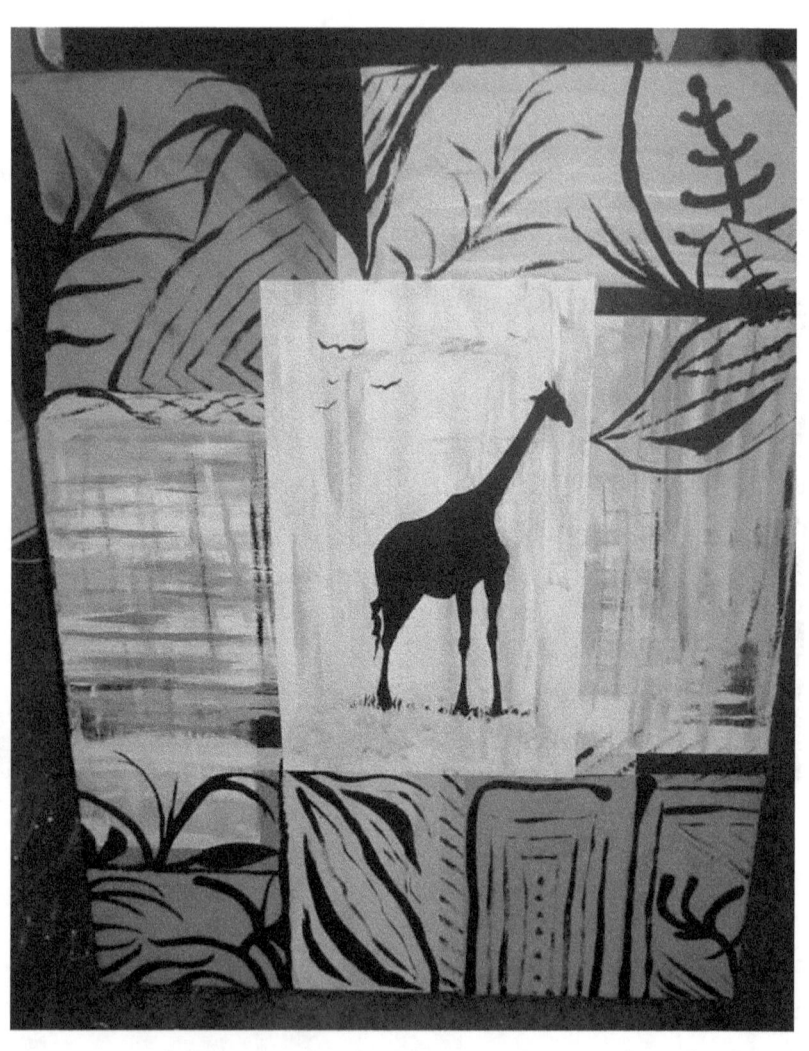

THE LEPOARD 2015

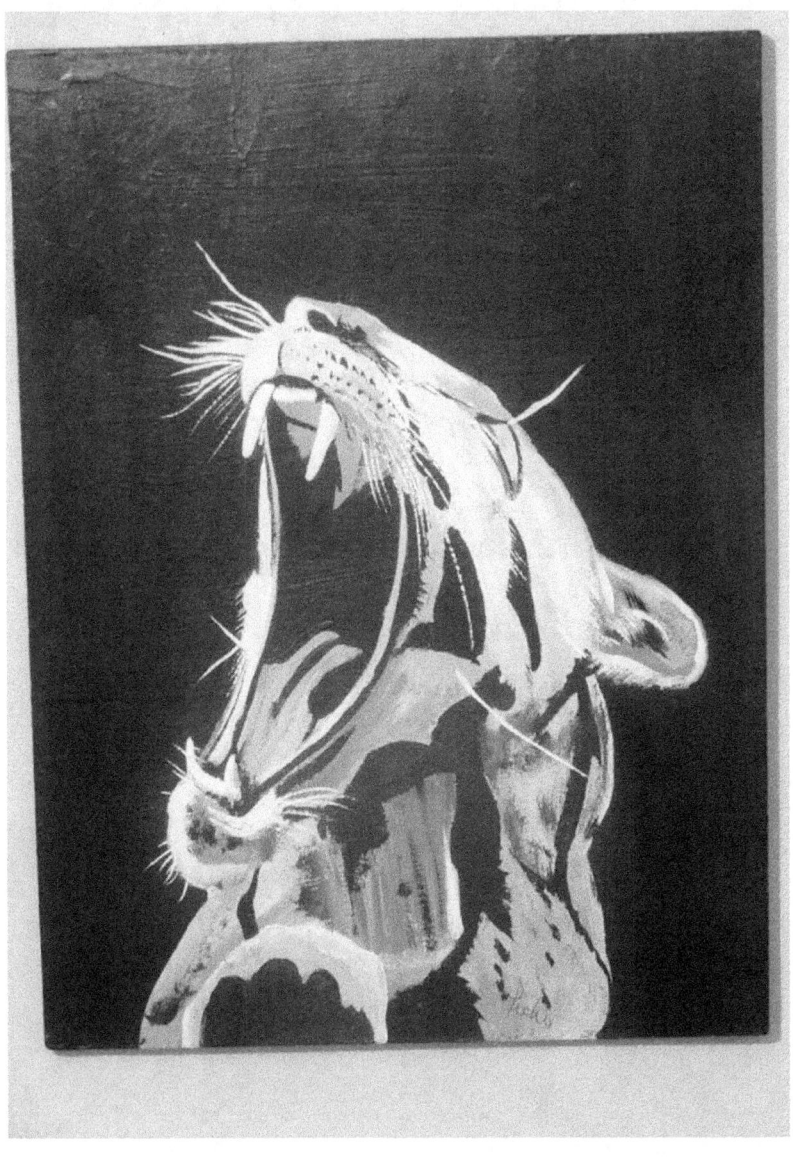

TRUE LOVE 2013

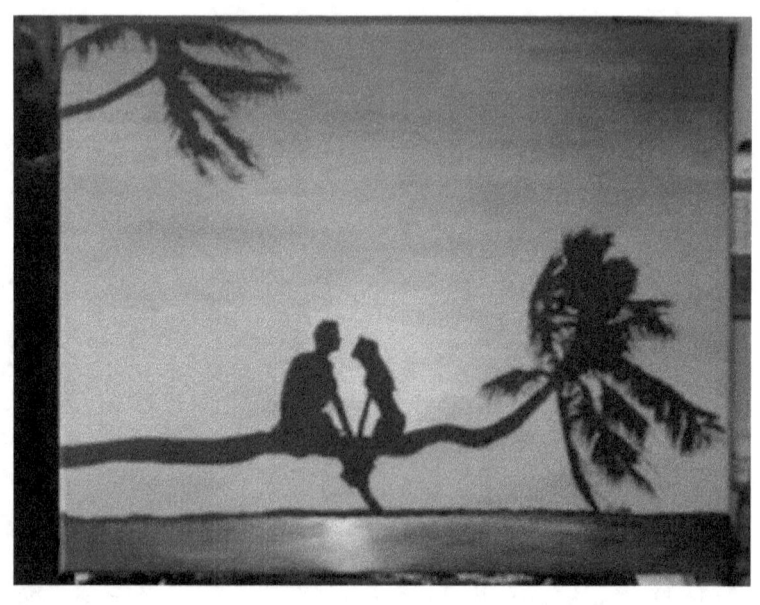

WILD FLOWER 2015

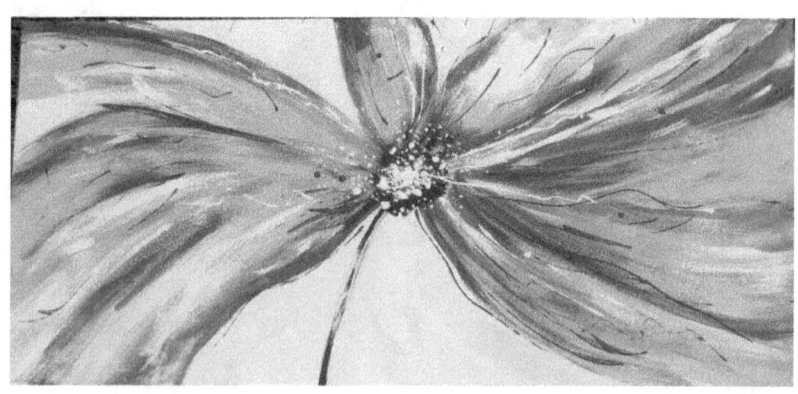

VALLEY WAY MURAL 2015

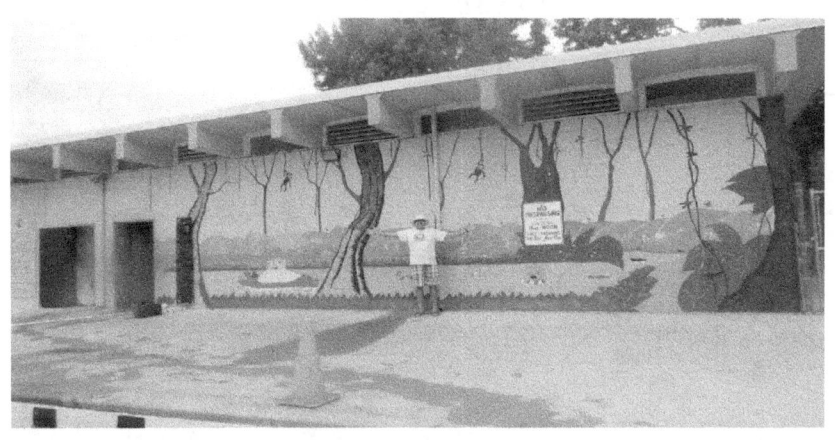

VALLEY POOL 2 2015

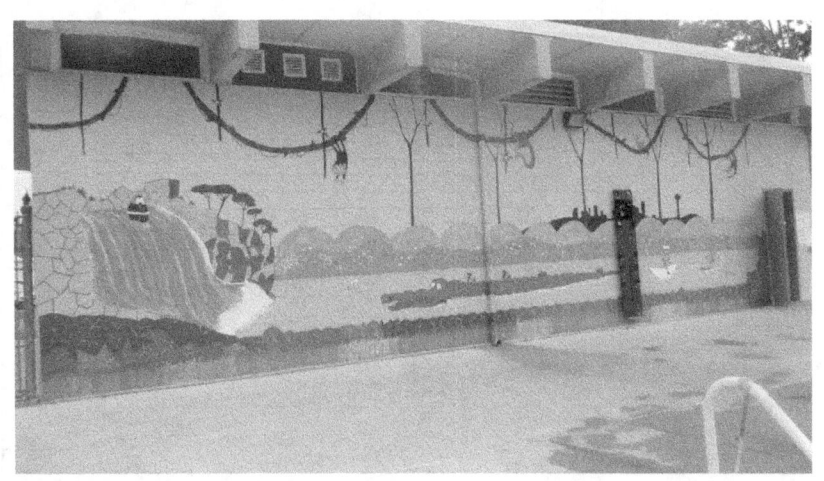

MONKEY 2014

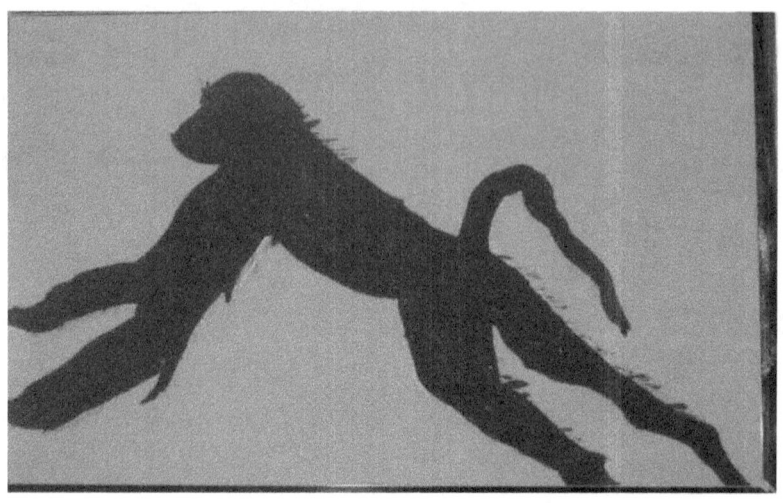

RINO 2014

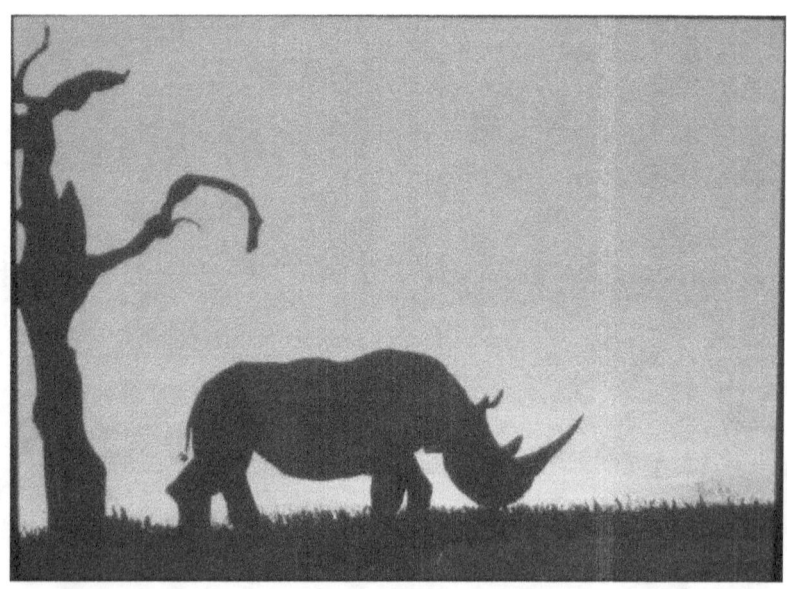

THE PARIE 2014

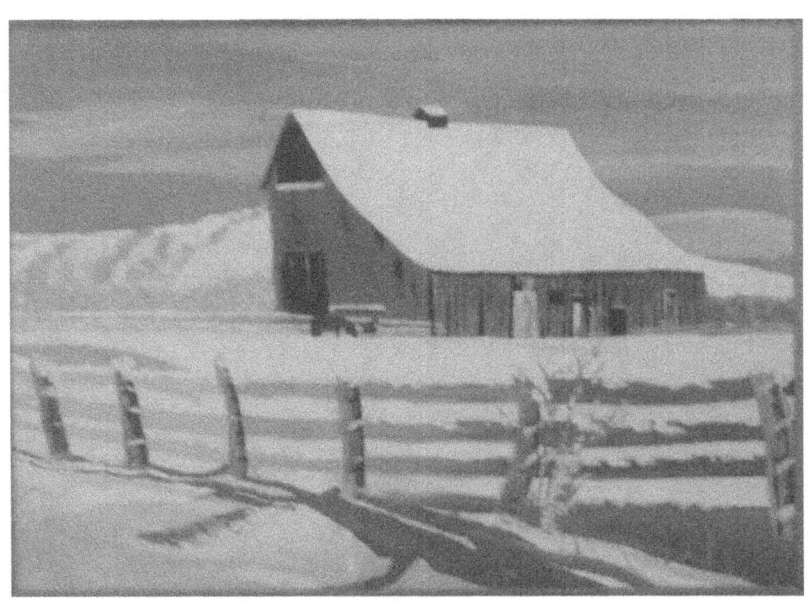

ZEBRA AT WORK 2015

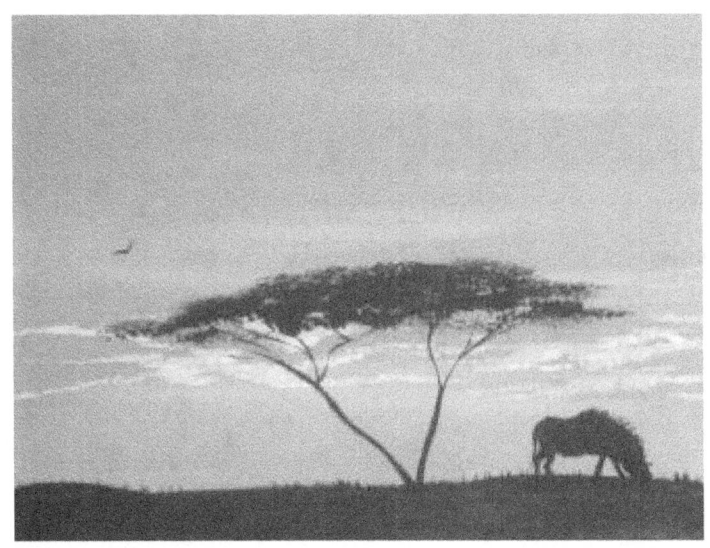

LIONESS 2015

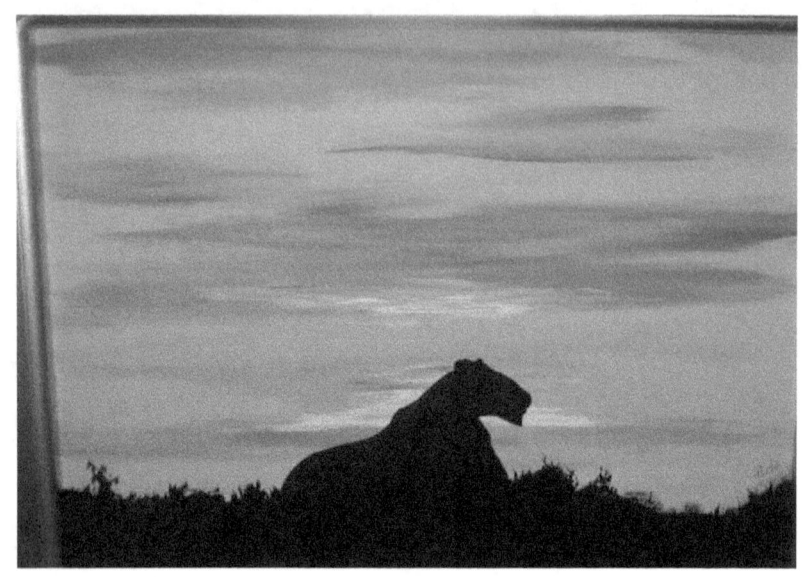

WATER BUFFALO 2015

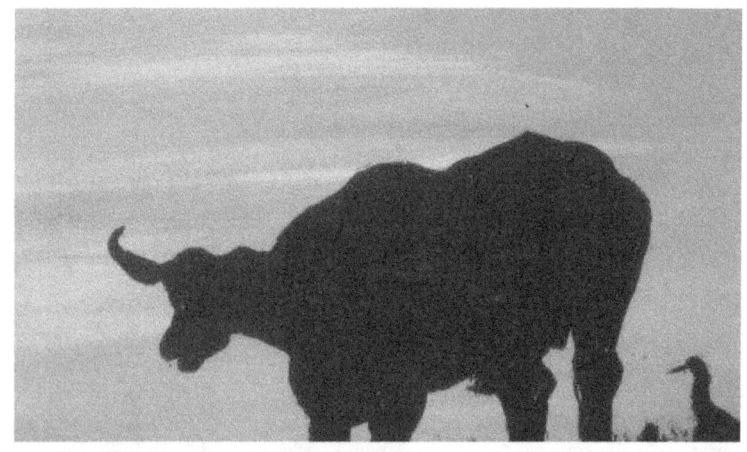

SUNSET 2015

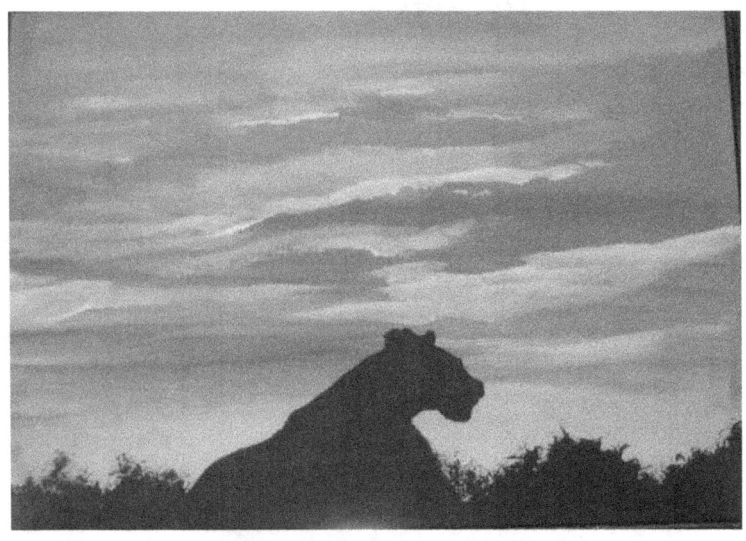

TIGER 2016

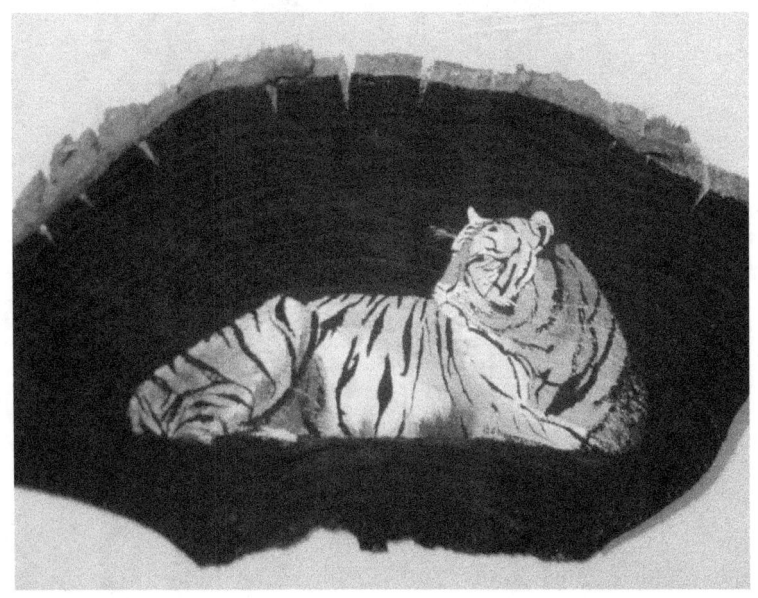

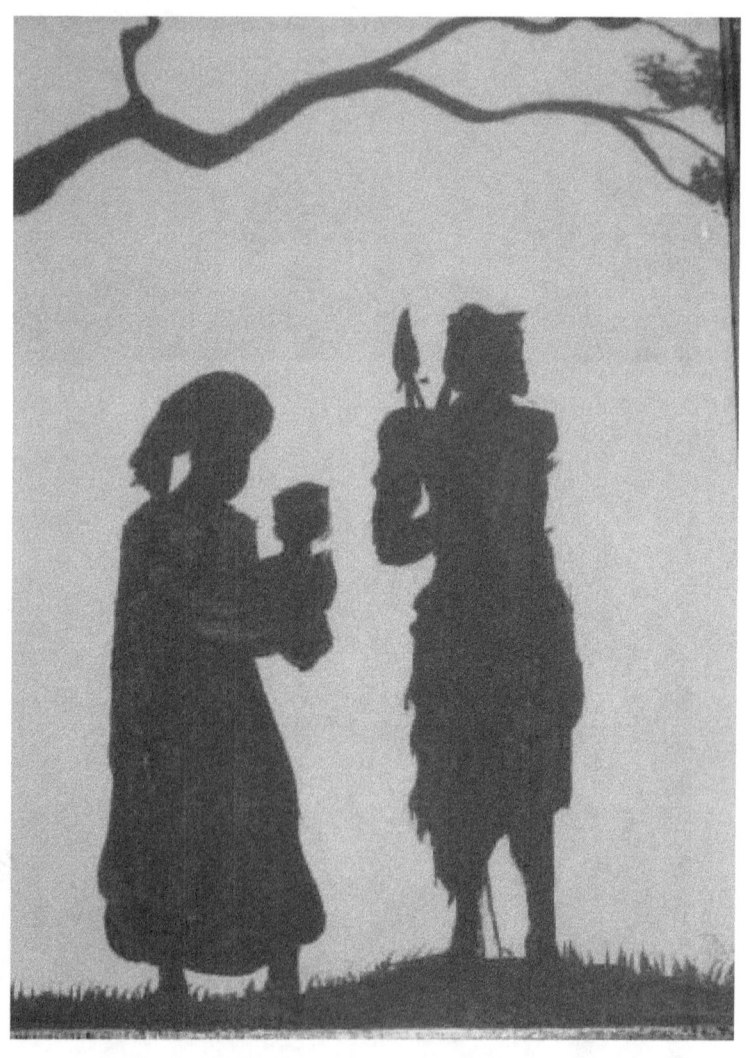

THE NORTHERN VALLEY 2015

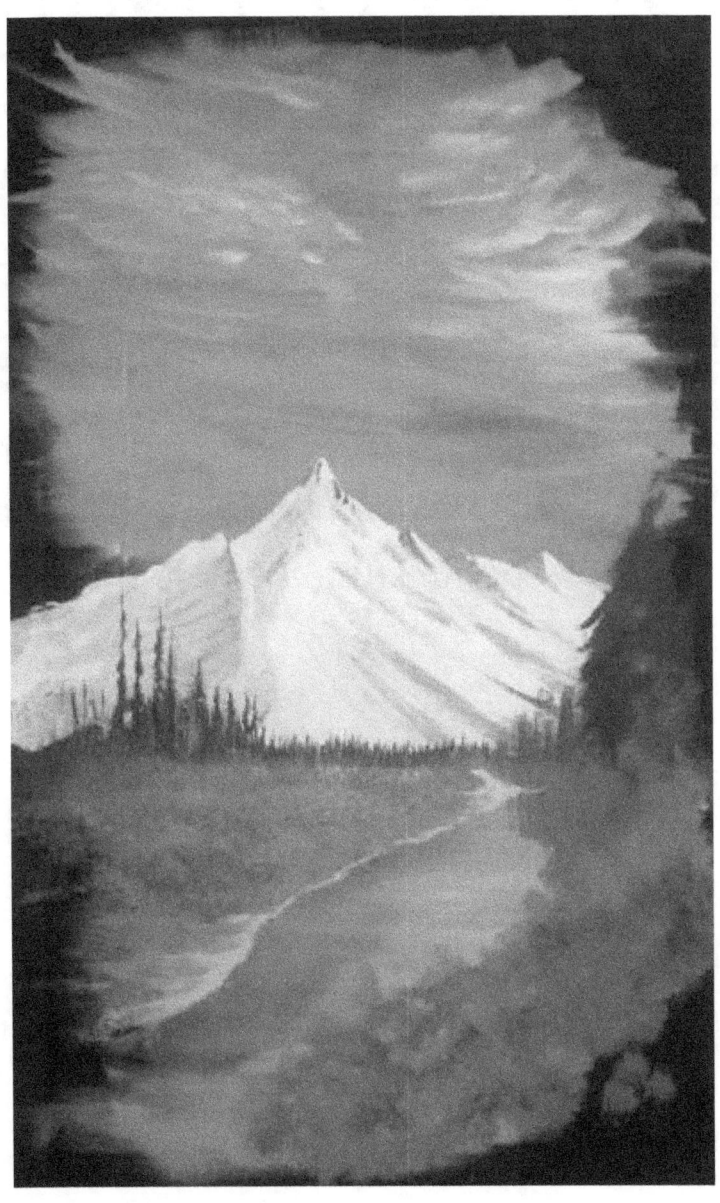

RIVER OF THE VALLEY 2014

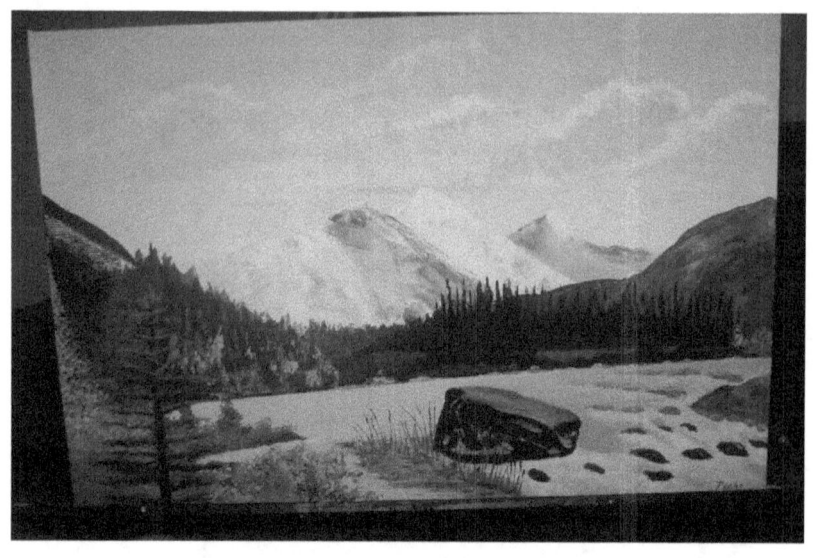

FLOWING RIVER 2013

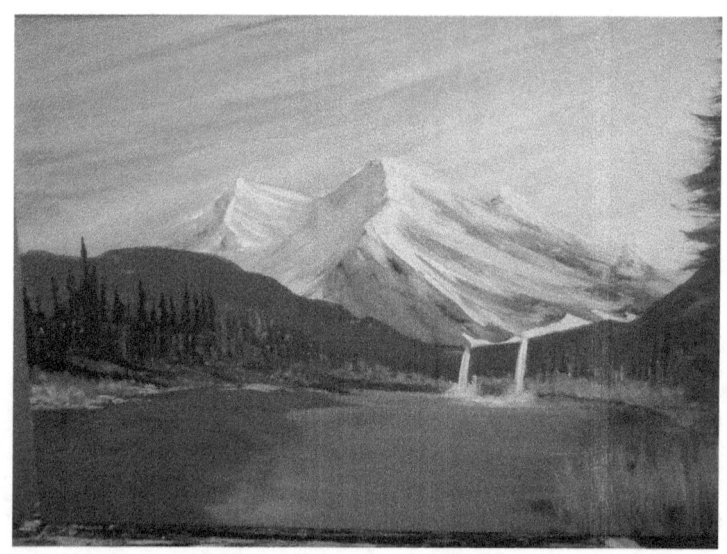

WINTER CALM 2015

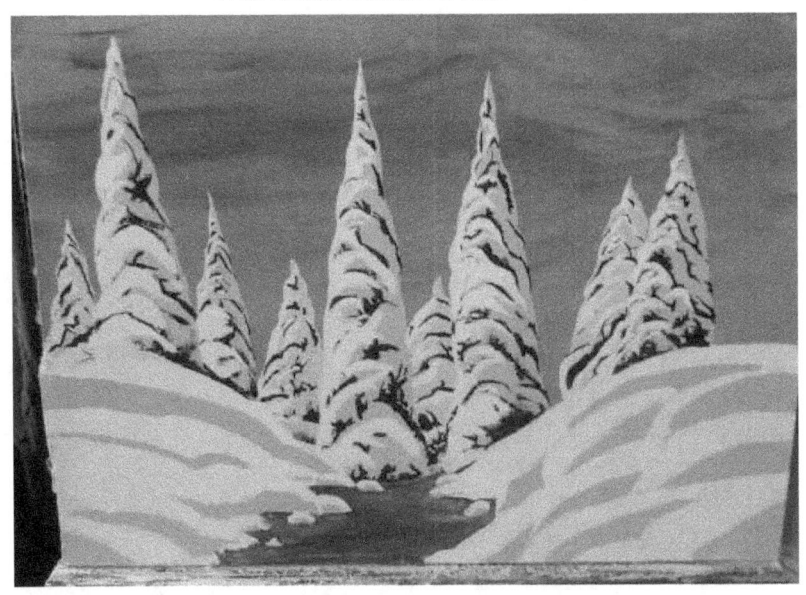

DRINKING WATER 2014

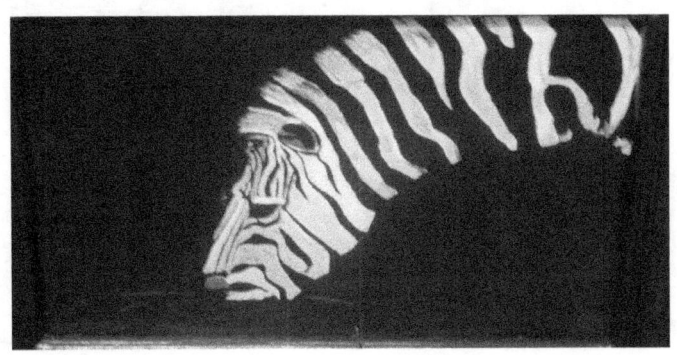

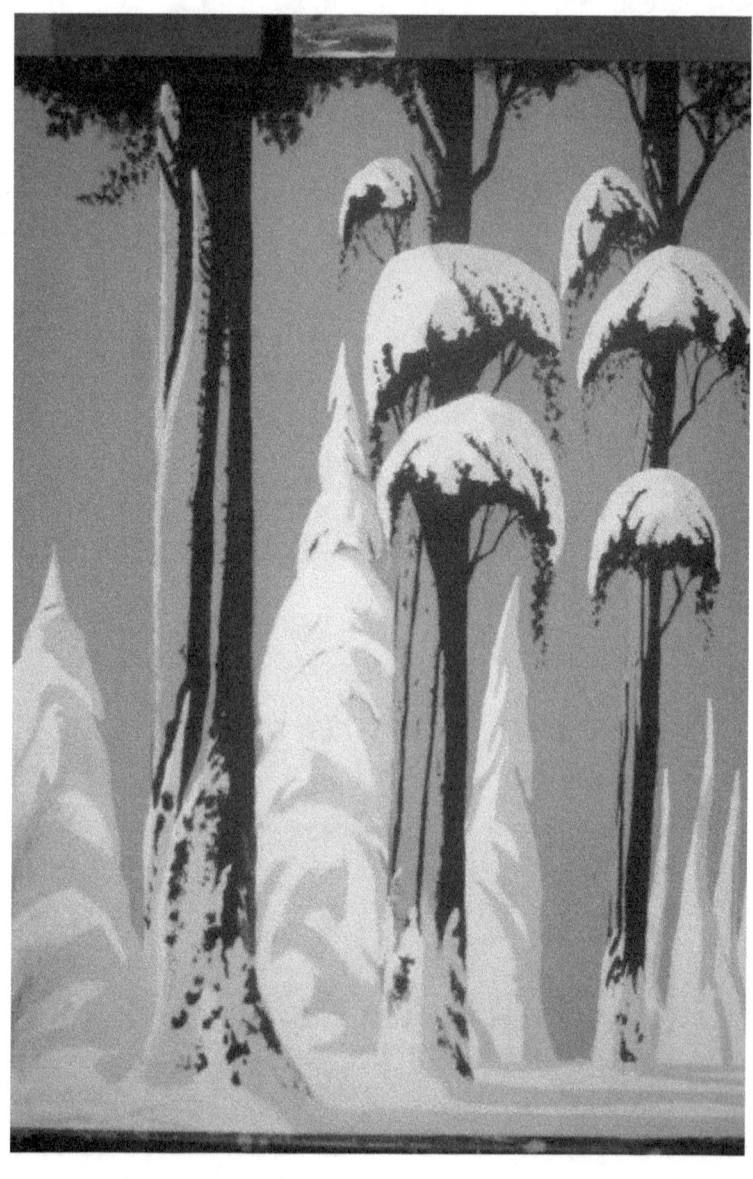

CHRISTMAS CHEERS 2015

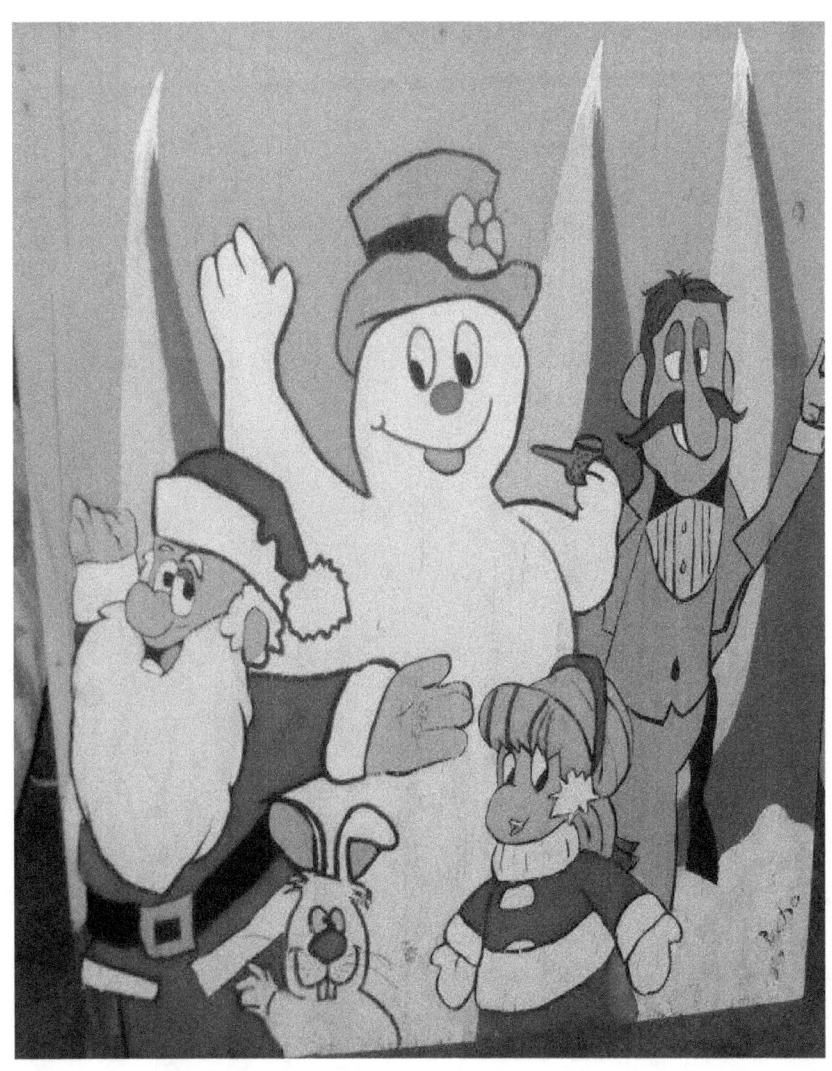

www.ingramcontent.com/pod-product-compliance
Lightning Source LLC
Chambersburg PA
CBHW071624170526
45166CB00003B/1179